WHAT THEY SAY ABOUT ALLAN FOTHERINGHAM

"Allan Fotheringham is a gifted and incisive writer. He wrote with penetrating insight and satire — often mischievous, almost never cruel. In private, Allan was caring and conscientious — sensitive to the feelings and problems of others, especially toward those who struggle with misfortune. The young and shy enjoyed his company because he was self-effacing, encouraging, and supportive toward those who were tentative and unsure in conversation in whatever context."

— THE RIGHT HONOURABLE EDWARD SCHREYER,
CANADA'S TWENTY-SECOND GOVERNOR GENERAL

"It is a little-known fact of Canadian journalism that I drew the illustrations *and* wrote the columns while Allan took frequent sabbaticals at the Betty Ford Clinic."

— ROY PETERSON,
CARTOONIST

"Dr. Foth, for decades, has surgically eviscerated his deserving political and other defenceless victims. What an accomplished life — showing what a fearless columnist/writer should be!"

— MICHAEL HARCOURT,
FORMER PREMIER OF BRITISH COLUMBIA

"Allan was our mother's favourite child. That's true. After his long, serious, and nearly fatal illness, I received a letter from Allan. In the envelope was one folded sheet of paper. In a recognizable scrawl were the words 'I'm back.' Following our frequent Saskatchewan family reunions, we lived in dread and fear of reading about ourselves and our outrageously exaggerated antics in the back page of *Maclean's*. Allan's long-time friend and cartoonist Roy Peterson always picked up the spirit of the occasion. Together they created Canadiana."

— IRENE McEOWN,
ALLAN FOTHERINGHAM'S SISTER

"Fotheringham's public reputation — the irreverent balloon-popper of the nation's gaseous elite — overshadowed his real gift. When he wanted to be, when he turned his eye to life outside the halls of power, he was the best pure writer columnizing in North America. It was that persona of Fotheringham I admired — not the ironist but the writer who found the heart of things. A poet lurked underneath that smirk, and I sometimes think that, to our loss, his ambition overtook his talent."
— PETE MCMARTIN,
VANCOUVER SUN COLUMNIST

"Allan Fotheringham is a deliciously subversive humour monger, a satirist with a mildly left-of-centre sensibility that he aims at pricking the bubbled-up egos of self-styled important people, usually politicians. In an inordinately polite and respectful country, his kind of wit is entertaining, refreshing, and absolutely essential, and he is one of Canada's best writers to boot."
— JOHN LAXTON,
VANCOUVER LAWYER AND DEVELOPER

"My brother, Allan, and I shared a bedroom for almost the first twenty years of our lives, he on the top bunk and me below. We shared the same clothes, played on the same athletic teams, and competed every day — one trying to outdo the other. But how in hell that tight relationship allowed him to share my earned doctorate, I will never know!"
— THE REAL DR. JOHN ("JACK") FOTHERINGHAM

"Allan Fotheringham is one of this country's superb journalists — honoured by his peers, feared by the powerful, respected by all who made it a habit to read his vivid observations, criticisms, and inspired opinions about the state of Canada and the lives of Canadians."
— ANNA PORTER,
AUTHOR OF *THE GHOSTS OF EUROPE*

Boy from Nowhere
A Life in Ninety-One Countries

ALLAN FOTHERINGHAM

DUNDURN
TORONTO

Editor: Michael Carroll
Design: Jesse Hooper
Printer: Transcontinental

Library and Archives Canada Cataloguing in Publication

Fotheringham, Allan, 1932-
    Boy from nowhere : a life in ninety-one countries / by Allan Fotheringham.

Issued also in electronic formats.
ISBN 978-1-4597-0168-7

    1. Fotheringham, Allan, 1932-. 2. Journalists--Canada--Biography. 3. Foreign correspondents--Canada--Biography. I. Title.

PN4913.F677A3 2011   070.92   C2011-903797-1

1   2   3   4   5   15   14   13   12   11

We acknowledge the support of the **Canada Council for the Arts** and the **Ontario Arts Council** for our publishing program. We also acknowledge the financial support of the **Government of Canada** through the **Canada Book Fund** and **Livres Canada Books,** and the **Government of Ontario** through the **Ontario Book Publishing Tax Credit** and the **Ontario Media Development Corporation.**

Care has been taken to trace the ownership of copyright material used in this book. The author and the publisher welcome any information enabling them to rectify any references or credits in subsequent editions.

J. Kirk Howard, President

Printed and bound in Canada.
www.dundurn.com

Dundurn	Gazelle Book Services Limited	Dundurn
3 Church Street, Suite 500	White Cross Mills	2250 Military Road
Toronto, Ontario, Canada	High Town, Lancaster, England	Tonawanda, NY
M5E 1M2	LA1 4XS	U.S.A. 14150

To my grandchildren,
Quinn, Lauren, Lachlan, Hunter, and Angus,
and their fun Uncle Brady.

ALSO BY ALLAN FOTHERINGHAM

Collected and Bound (1972)

The World According to Roy Peterson: With the Gospel According to Allan Fotheringham (1979)

Malice in Blunderland — Or How the Grits Stole Christmas (1982)

Look, Ma, No Hands: An Affectionate Look at Our Wonderful Tories (1983)

Capitol Offences: Dr. Foth Meets Uncle Sam (1986)

Birds of a Feather: The Press and the Politicians (1989)

Last Page First (1999)

Fotheringham's Fictionary of Facts & Follies (2001)

Contents

Preface 9

1   Hello, World 13

2   To the Garden of Eden 21

3   Campus Chaff 31

4   To Warsaw on a Scooter 40

5   London Town 49

6   Newspaper Madness 56

7   Vancouver and Marriage 59

8   Twenty-Six Libel Writs 69

9   Hitting $492,000 78

10   *Toronto Sun* Days 89

11   2000 Was a Busy Year 99

12   Conquering Africa 108

13   Me and Mulroney 111

14   Pierre Elliott Himself 115

15   The Reluctant Queen 122

16   I Meet the Gem 125

17   On to Hollywood 134

18   You Wanna Be a Journalist? ... 140

19   Death Beckons 143

20   My Female Friends 148

21   From a Man I Had Never Met ... 152

22   My Greatest Accomplishment ... 157

23   And Then There's %$#&*!! ... 166

24   The Bohemian Grove 169

25   Watershed 173

26   Bowen Island 176

27   Cast of Characters 179

28   Life Is a Series of Memories ... 213

29   Fothisms 225

30   The First Page Last 227

31   Left on the Copy Room Floor ... 231

Preface

I have often thought that you write an autobiography when your career is over. However, writers never really retire. At least I haven't. I am seventy-nine years old and have recently written for *The Roughneck*, a magazine out of Calgary; have blogged for *Zoomer* magazine (yes, I blog and twitter); occasionally write for the *Globe and Mail* and the *National Post*; and submit columns to *Maclean's*.

I am not bored. I play tennis three times a week at 9:00 a.m. with what I fondly call the "Geezer Group" at my tennis club and am still on the speakers' circuit. I have three great children and five wonderful grandchildren who keep me coming to Vancouver to see them and, in the process, many of my long-standing friends. My lovely wife, Anne, and I travel on a regular basis and know many people around the world.

I have journeyed to some ninety-one countries in the course of my career and am planning to add to that number. I have received two honorary degrees and numerous awards. And I am proud to say I have been fired by every major newspaper and news agency in Canada. I have met Joe Louis, Zhou Enlai, Robert F. Kennedy, Henry Kissinger, Nikita Khrushchev, Bill Clinton, Pierre Elliott Trudeau, Vladimir Putin, Nelson Mandela, Mickey Mantle, Brian Mulroney, Jean Chrétien, Paul Martin, Stephen Harper, Pope John Paul II, Diana, Princess of Wales,

The head table at the Bob Edwards Award 25th anniversary luncheon in Calgary in 1999. Left to right: myself, June Callwood, David Suzuki, and Margaret Atwood. I received the award in 1990.

Queen Elizabeth II (thrice), Prince Charles, Prince Philip, Muhammad Ali, Shimon Peres, Louis Armstrong, Bob Hunter, and The Beatles, to name a few.

So why now? Because in 2007 I got a wake-up call. I went in for a routine colonoscopy, and due to medical error, did not come out of the hospital for four months. I almost died more than once, had the last rites performed, and am here only due to the efforts of my wife, who spent one hundred and forty-five days in the hospital for ten hours a day wearing a hospital gown, a face mask, and gloves while helping me and monitoring what was occurring. I was in rehab for a year, and after another operation to replace a knee and another year of rehab, I am healthy and here to tell the tale.

When something like this happens, you realize how fragile life is and how easily it can be taken away from you. And until now I haven't sat down to write about my life so that my grandchildren, Quinn, Lauren, Lachlan, Hunter, and Angus, will know about their "Oompah." Sure, they can look up my old columns. My readers know that over the years I have written about where I was or what I have been doing among other things. My readers know more about me than my grandchildren do. So this is for them. In the process I hope you, the reader, obtain more insight into me and my life, as well.

A Special Note from the Author

During the editing of this book, my number one son, Brady, died in Seoul, South Korea, where he had been living for eight years. He had a massive heart attack and died instantly. At only forty-seven.

Brady was an adventurer until the day he died. The last time I spoke with him he was telling me about all of the books he was reading as research on the Middle East. He felt he had conquered Asia and was determined to go to all of the Middle Eastern countries. I was very impressed with his knowledge of these nations. Brady never did anything by half.

My wife, Anne, was speaking to Brady just prior to his heading out for work when he had the heart attack in his apartment. They were discussing his holidays, which were coming up in the next few weeks, and his visa application form for entry into Syria at a time when the newspapers were reporting numerous deaths each day due to the conflict there. A conflict in a country never phased Brady.

He was then planning to go on to Lebanon. Not London … Lebanon.

When you read this book, you will find how special Brady was. He was the bravest person I ever met. I will miss him terribly.

Boy from Nowhere is not only dedicated to my five grandchildren but to my son, Brady.

1
Hello, World

I never knew my father. He died when I was two. I have been amused all my life by the accusation — my mother was the strongest person I have ever encountered and I had two older sisters — that I prefer the company of females to the male species. I find most men dull.

I am a Saskatchewan boy. I was born in Rouleau Hospital at the height of the Depression on August 31, 1932. Rouleau (later the site of TV's *Corner Gas*) was the closest town with a hospital. Hearne, where my family lived, is fifty miles south of Regina. People from Hearne are called "Hearnias." In fact, the town was so small it couldn't afford a village idiot. Everyone had to take turns.

The population of Hearne was twenty-six: one street, one general store, one blacksmith shop, a church, and two grain elevators. As with most of rural Saskatchewan, there was no running water, no electricity. The name comes with appropriate heritage — named after Sir Samuel Hearne, who joined the Royal Navy as a captain's batman at age eleven and was knighted after becoming the first European explorer to reach the Arctic overland, and then spent his final days in a Paris prison.

My mother, Edna, was one of eleven children of the Clarke farm family. She had seven brothers (Dick, Jim, Dale, Harvey, Jack, Les, and Lloyd) and three sisters (Dora, Ruby, and Irene). Having married young at nineteen, something everyone tended to do on the Prairies during the Depression, Edna had four children in five years. I was the third in line, first son.

On the day of my birth, three of her seven brothers set out in a truck to drive her the seventeen miles to Rouleau. There hadn't been any rain on the Prairies for three years. It was as dry as a bone. The ground was like icing sugar. When it finally did rain, it was like chocolate fudge. They called it "gumbo mud." Needless to say, it rained the night of the truck ride. A mickey of rye accompanied the three soon-to-be uncles on the trip. It was tough going.

Boy from Nowhere

The truck went into the ditch four times because of the gumbo, while my mother was moaning in the back. And then it happened. The sky went completely black. It was a total eclipse of the sun. They didn't know what to make of it but carried on, eventually getting to the hospital.

Once I came into the world, the brothers crept into my mother's hospital room and asked what she was going to name me. "Murray Allan," she replied.

"Shucks," said Uncle Jack, "we were hoping you were going to call him 'Gumbo Eclipse.'" (In later life I thought that would have made a great byline in the *New York Times*: "By Gumbo Eclipse Fotheringham.")

I heard the story of my birth many times from my mother. I always thought that with time the story became exaggerated. However, many decades later, a girlfriend of mine, Marilyn Freer, gave me a very special gift — a leather-bound copy of the *New York Times* on the day I was born. There on the front page was the story and a map about the total eclipse of the sun that occurred across the continent, including that gumbo road to Rouleau. I apologized to my mother for ever doubting her story. In retrospect it all seemed fitting.

I was named after James Allan, my great-grandfather. Here is his story.

With my siblings Donna, Irene, and Jack in front of our home in Hearne, Saskatchewan. I have on the long pants and the funny hat.

Hello, World

In 1845, James Allan, seventeen years old, and his younger brother, William Allan, aged fifteen, lived as orphans with an aunt and uncle in Antrim, Ireland. They suffered a miserable existence that prompted them to run away to the Port of Belfast. Somehow they managed to board a sailing ship and hide themselves as stowaways.

The uncle discovered their departure and traced their disappearance to the sailing ship. Along with the captain, he searched the vessel and apprehended William, the younger brother. James Allan wasn't found, and thus sailed away as a stowaway, arriving in Canada penniless and homeless.

This was the parting of the two Allan brothers.

A history tells us that they did eventually establish a correspondence by mail, but it had been neglected in the later days of their lives.

Great-Grandfather James Allan started a career in the lumber trades. First, he hauled logs by oxen, then eventually he had his own sawmill powered by steam. James Allan died in 1905, spending his last years living in Ontario among his family of seven children. He was buried in a cemetery in Shelburne, Ontario.

William, the younger brother, spent his career in the British military, serving in many parts of the world, including the newly developing territory of Canada. Despite his diligent inquiries and search for his brother, James, they were never together again. On the death of Great-Grandfather James Allan, a chance contact was made by his offspring to their Uncle William. He was then brought to Canada from England and lived out his remaining years with the children of his brother.

Upon his death in 1911, William was buried in the same plot with his brother in the cemetery in Shelburne. Finally, the Allan brothers were together again after sixty-five years. (A coincidence of life is that three generations later, my son, Kip, is in the timber business.)

My mother was three weeks from her twenty-fourth birthday when I was born. Brother Jack came a year later. My father, John Scott, ran the local grocery store. I have been told by my aunts that he was a fine man and that he and my mother were madly in love. I don't remember him; as mentioned earlier, he was rude enough to die when I was two. He died in my mother's arms in Rouleau Hospital after a botched appendectomy. He was thirty-one.

His death shattered my mother's life. Here she was, twenty-six, with four children under the age of five in the heart of the Prairies in the middle of the Depression. How could this tragedy happen to two people who were so happy with each other? It toughened her. It gave her an inner strength she never knew she had. In order to support the family, she took in washing. Because she had taken violin lessons in high school, she was able to give lessons for 50 cents an hour. Half the students couldn't pay.

The post office needed someone to run it for the area. My mother took on the position and turned our house into the local mail stop for the farm families that surrounded the hamlet. Ottawa paid her $35 a month. With the help of her father who had the farm, she was able to get fresh vegetables and milk, and so we got by.

As a child, I was fascinated by what was placed in the small boxes in the post office. Mother filled these wickets from the kitchen side of our house. After she stuffed the wickets with the mail, I snuck out the magazines and flipped through them, making sure to put them back before the rightful owners came to collect them. On more than one occasion, I retrieved an atlas and put it on the floor, leafing through various

My parents' wedding day in Saskatchewan — everyone in their Sunday best.

continents, telling my mother that someday I would go to all of those places. And I have.

When it was time to go to school, my sisters, Donna and Irene, and my brother, Jack, and I travelled three miles to Amherst, a one-room schoolhouse in the countryside. During the winter, Mother drove us in the Plymouth. When the weather got warm enough, we walked home, cutting across the wheat fields. Irene remembers that I always walked a half-mile behind the three of them. Many years later she said, "We knew then that you were the *weird* one."

There were thirty kids spread over grades one to nine. Only two were in grades one, two, and three — Kenny Newans and me. Kenny, skinny and undernourished, came from a big family. I remember that his folks were so poor that each of them would bring white bread slices with lard in the middle to make a sandwich. That constituted lunch.

Kenny grew up to become sports director of a Calgary TV station. Two children in the same grade out in the middle of nowhere and both eventually going into the media business. How strange.

One of the major projects Kenny and I worked on was to snare gophers. First thing in the morning, the teacher handed out assignments to each grade. When they were finished, we were allowed to go outside. Kenny and I were prepared. We had binder twine and water ready for the catch. The field by the school had plenty of gopher holes. One of us poured water down a hole while the other was ready at the other end of the tunnel. When the soaking-wet gopher poked its head out of his hole, he was snared by the binder-twine noose.

After we snared two gophers, we took them back to the classroom and tied them to the legs of our desks. As Kenny and I sat across the aisle from each other, we watched and manipulated them as the gophers fought furiously. To us it was great sport. No wonder Kenny became a successful sports director.

Of course, there was always a scandal in a school so small. In those days in the Depression, there was no money to pay the schoolteacher, who was usually a woman. So one of the farm families provided her with room and board. That was her pay. The farm families were very protective of the teacher. After all, she was responsible for their darlings' education.

Boy from Nowhere

Our teacher, Lillian Moen, at the end of one school day was in the barn outside where the schoolboys put their ponies each morning. One of the boys (I think it was Uncle Dick, who was in grade eight) took a stick and, showing off in front of his pals, stuck it up the back of Miss Moen's skirt. This, as could be imagined, was the scandal of all scandals in the community.

One day we little guys in grade one or two were astounded, not knowing anything about the incident, to see all of the senior boys, including Uncle Dick, go to the front of the room and apologize one by one to Miss Moen. Their fathers had heard about the deed and laid on the punishment. My Uncle Dick never mentioned that day to his death. (No wonder he was my favourite uncle.)

And, like today, when school kids watch a hotshot pull into the school parking lot with a Ferrari or a Porsche, we little kids gawked at the big boys as they came in on their ponies. The star was a guy who rode a pinto stallion pony, black and white, which snorted and had wild eyes and was hard to control. That guy was the star like the kid with the Porsche today.

My first recollection as a young child (about three or four) was of a large cactus across the only street in Hearne. I said to my younger brother, Jack (who must have been two or three), "Let's see who can sit down closest to the cactus. You go first." I can almost remember thinking at the time: *How dumb can you be to take that offer?*

As soon as he squatted, I, of course, shoved him into the cactus. He ran screaming home, and my mother almost killed me as she had to pluck out all the offending needles. That was the start of a long-standing feud between Jack and me.

Jack and I once played on the same basketball team at high school in British Columbia. When we went to practice from our home three miles away, I stood fifty yards distant from him hitchhiking, and he had to hitch a ride with a different car. I was captain of the team then, and when we came out on the floor, we had to pass to each other before hitchhiking home again separately.

We shared bunk beds, and once during a disagreement, I took all his clothes and threw them out the bedroom window onto the roof while it was raining. At one point, for a whole year, we didn't say a word to each other. A feat unto itself since we shared the same bedroom, and bunk beds at that. (I suppose it was due to the Irish blood we had both inherited — Northern Ireland Protestant, of course.)

When I was supposedly a grown-up adult, I asked Mother why she thought Jack and I fought so much. She surprised me with a very calm, reflective answer. "Because," she said without a moment's hesitation, "without a father in your lives, you were fighting for the attention of your mother." I thought that was a very wise (if obvious) Freudian statement.

It is said that when you lose your father at a very young age, your mother becomes your whole universe. The bond between the children and surviving parent becomes greater than if there are two parents. The parent gathers strength due to the children, and the children rely solely on the surviving parent. To this day, I think my mother has had the greatest influence on my life. She was not only the strongest woman I have ever met, as I have mentioned, she was also the strongest person I have ever met.

As is the nature of growing up, all children innocently experiment with sex. In my case, one day when I was about eight, all four of us were out and saw two dogs "doing it." A group of men stood around watching and laughing and using appropriate words to describe what was going on. We all came home and mother was out. When she returned, I was lying naked on top of a naked Irene who was on a circular carpet in one of the bedrooms. My mother shouted, "What are you doing!"

I said, "We are fucking," having just learned this new word from the men. Fade to black.

Eight years went by before my mother was noticed by the only bachelor in Hearne. His name was Doug Fotheringham, and he lived across the street. He was a quiet man, religious and a teetotaler — apparently because his father was a bad drinker. Before long they became an item. We were mother's world, and she was ours. I didn't think there was any room for this intruder.

The courtship wasn't hurried; there was no need to hurry. The family rule was that the first daughter to marry inherited the family china. Since my mother had previously jumped the queue by marrying my father, she already had the "family jewels," which angered her sisters.

However, the day came when Mr. Fotheringham joined the Canadian Army at the start of the Second World War and was to be transferred to Regina (they couldn't transfer him to anywhere else on the bald prairie). I don't know whatever possessed him to take on four brats, but he proposed to my mother and she accepted. Although my sisters disagreed with me, I felt that my mother wasn't so much "in love" with him but married him to get us out of Hearne and not become dirt farmers. I was wrong. Her mature love for him in later years was apparent to everyone.

Memories of Hearne? I still remember Grandfather Clarke on the farm, calling out "Jim … I mean, Dale … uh, Jack … no, Dick … er, Lloyd …" before finally settling on who he was looking for: "Les!"

What does a boy remember? Getting left behind at a Hearne church picnic at the Moose Jaw Zoo and winning three races and 75 cents at an adjoining church picnic until rescuers from Hearne arrived back hours later. A survivor? Hint of a future life path?

And the most evocative memory of all, that tells everything about Saskatchewan in the Depression years: of weeding in the cornfields at Grandpa Clarke's farm and whenever a car went by — perhaps two or three in a day a good fifty yards away on the road — there would be an instant wave from whoever it was, a total stranger, and all the kids in the field would wave back wildly. A very lonely land but a very friendly land.

2
To the Garden of Eden

As I mentioned, Regina is fifty miles north of Hearne. For a nine-year-old that was like going from Kansas to Manhattan. But my world became my new school, the unfortunately named Wetmore Elementary where I entered grade three. I had an early interest in school games, which were a precursor to my interest in sports. At recess and noon hour the favourite game was dodge ball. Because I was so quick on my feet, I always won. This was a good game that stood me in good stead when, in the future, I had to dodge arrows in the journalism business.

But, by a fluke, and this was a formative thing in my life, there was a public library just doors down from our home on Broder Street. I was raised in a house without books. The only thing I had to read as I grew up was *Chatelaine* and *Ladies' Home Journal*. (Some clue to my later understanding of women?) I discovered this library and took out two

This is where it all began.

books a week, all by the same author. They were about the collie Lad of Sunnybank by Albert Payson Terhune.

Years later in journalism I was accused of using commas too much. The other day I found an old copy of *Lad of Sunnybank* in which my beloved author writes: "Lad, getting up in the morning, would delight in the sunshine, before he went down to the creek, to look at the cattle." I laughed my head off because I could see how I had fallen in love with commas. It was *his* fault.

At school the other kids always asked: "Why is your name Scott and your family's name Fotheringham?" So my stepfather decided to legally adopt us and change our surname. I didn't like the idea. But at the age of nine, I didn't have much clout. I was no longer Murray Allan Scott. Years later I read about a Brooklyn boy who was born Bernard Schwartz who was going nowhere as an actor until Hollywood changed his name to Tony Curtis. Roy Harold Scherer, Jr., became Rock Hudson. Archibald Leach? Cary Grant. Not to mention Norma Jeane Mortenson later Baker — Marilyn Monroe.

When I got into newspapering, the byline Allan Fotheringham had a faint rhyming sound to it, a name easy to remember as it turned out. Murray Scott? Dead meat. I was lucky, as usual.

Doug Fotheringham, with a high school education, must have been very good at numbers, because he rose swiftly in the Canadian Army and became a paymaster and Captain Fotheringham. The army told him they were transferring him to Camp Chilliwack, sixty-five miles east of Vancouver in far-off British Columbia, and since he was a non-fighting soldier, just signing cheques, he asked if he could move his family to British Columbia, assuming he would be there for the rest of the war. He did so, and the army, being the army, immediately shipped him overseas.

That meant my mother, happily married, became a "widow" once again for the rest of the war. Years later my mother told me the story of Doug writing home from overseas and warning her to take a good look at the walls because when he got home she would only see the ceiling. I think this was the standard joke among soldiers and was written to dozens of brides left behind.

By the time Doug returned, I, of course, was a snotty-nosed teenager and out of control. I wasn't going to take any guff from a guy I hardly knew.

This caused problems. I can remember one supper when the tension was such that not a single word was spoken throughout the meal between four children, my mother, and my stepfather.

When Doug first arrived in British Columbia, he answered an ad in the *Chilliwack Progress*, the local weekly, which said that a family would take in a soldier — "non-drinking and non-smoking." So he went to the famed home of Oliver Wells, who had geese and cattle and was a world-renowned breeder and corresponded with people of his ilk around the globe. They had a house for a farmhand on the property and said it could accommodate his family of four children and a wife. We took a train, never having been on one before, from Regina and travelled forever over the Rocky Mountains, seeing raging rivers and deep canyons and snowy peaks. Being from the flat prairie, we had never seen a hill.

We arrived on a Saturday morning and took a ferry across the Fraser River. At the Wells estate, which was called Edenbank, there were cattle a-sloshing in the Luk-a-Kuk Stream below a huge home with large Canadian geese strolling across a lawn. It was fall, and lush apples and pears were falling from trees in the brilliant sunshine. I actually thought we had arrived in the Garden of Eden. I was ten years old.

The Wells family was what one would call these days the Establishment. They introduced my mother to the Carman United Church. The small town of Sardis, perhaps two hundred souls, was divided into those who went to church and the heathens who didn't. My mother, who had a musical background, having taught violin at the age of seventeen in Hearne, was embraced in this ambience and wound up leading the choir for forty years. My sister, Donna, sang in the choir. Doug, when he came home from the war with his swift knowledge of figures, became church treasurer. It was the essence, the country club of this little town. You either belonged to it or you didn't. It was the pillar of my mother's life for the rest of her ninety-seven years.

We were forced to go to Sunday School every week accompanied by our mongrel dog Butch, who followed us, and being a religious dog, waited faithfully outside every Sunday. I, cutting out from church after Sunday School, was assigned to go home and put in the oven the ritual Sunday roast of beef. Often I stopped at the local basketball hall (Butch dutifully waiting at the entrance), perfecting skills that were going to take me to the Olympics, and forgot to go home. My parents would arrive back from church with the stove not on and the roast not arriving until two hours later. These weren't happy moments.

There was one stretch where I didn't miss Sunday School for five years. I received medals for this achievement, which I can produce today. I was also once directed to sit down and sign a formal pledge (I was twelve years old!) that liquor wouldn't cross my lips forever. Such are the dreams of adult Christians.

However, in the same church some years later, I fainted while my brother and his wife were having the christening of their first child. I had been out rather late the previous evening in Vancouver, and my sister, Irene, and her husband had to wake me up for the sixty-five-mile drive to the ceremony in Sardis. Me, with no breakfast, noticed in the middle of singing a hymn that the words in the hymn book seemed to go fuzzy. I couldn't understand this, and the next thing I knew I went crashing down in my pew. Sister Donna, who was in the choir, and stepfather Doug, also in the choir, rushed down and escorted me out to the fresh air to revive me quickly. My brother, whose proud moment this was, has never quite forgiven me.

I attended Sardis Elementary, across the road from Edenbank. What a change from Hearne where we often walked the three miles. This was a hundred yards. There was a game in which the kids got down on hands and knees and tried to somersault over one another without touching each other. I used to win all the time since I could somersault over twelve kids.

At recess I also used to amuse the whole gang. There was a wimp called Jimmy Block, who I beat up. Oddly, he enjoyed it. Everyone watched while I ripped off his clothes and threw them up a tree. When the bell rang to signal the end of recess, he had to scramble up the tree to get his clothes. Thus he was always late for class and the teacher always asked why he was late. It was amusing at the time, but — hello there, Dr. Freud — it isn't one of my proudest memories. I have often wondered what happened to Jimmy Block. I have never heard from him.

One day for some crazy reason I ran away from home. I slept in the hayloft of a barn. The town was so small that the word got around and my parents knew where I was. They decided to wait me out. It lasted two days, and they were the victors. I now thoroughly understand the strategy of a SWAT team. Lack of food and sleep works every time.

At the end of the year, when we were in grade six before going to Chilliwack Junior High School, my teacher said we would be taking either one of two directions. Either a university entrance program or a general program. She openly said to students what program each would be taking. "Lorraine [who was the smartest person in the class], you will be going into the university program. Allan, you will, as well…." There were four of us who made the cut. The rest, in her mind, were going to be placed in the general program. No hope for the rest of them. Just us four.

My first step to the heights of journalism was in the *United Church Observer*, a national journal for all its churches across the country. The paper awarded prizes for the juvenile section. I sent in a poem about a castle in Spain. I have no idea how I picked that. I won first prize. The prize? Five dollars. I was a pro. I was in grade five. I was ten. The poem had a very idealistic, romantic theme. Here it is:

The Castle

High on a hill, the castle stands
The home of knights from many lands

Lonely and desolate, still she lies
The mark between the earth and skies

Witness of furious fights galore
Which reached right to the strong oak door.

Many attacks her defenders stood,
Fighting on though smeared with blood.
Sentries no longer pace the walls,
Nor knights and earls feast in the halls.

Boy from Nowhere

Now this fortress lies in ruins,
Stone arches now a cave for bruins;

Surrounded by an empty moat,
Now the pasture for a goat,

The castle, all her glory taken,
Lies empty, quiet and forsaken.

I find it funny that my start in a writing career was on a romantic theme and that I am now regarded as a cynic due to my satiric approach to politics and politicians. I also find it interesting that sixty-one years later my lovely seven-year-old granddaughter, Quinn, wrote her first short story on a romantic theme (set in a castle) and at age ten won the opportunity to have one of her poems published in a book in which the poetry was chosen from across the nation. Subsequently, my other beautiful granddaughter, Lauren, has published both her poetry and a short story.

At the end of grade six we took the school bus to Chilliwack Junior High, three miles away. On the first day, when we went into woodwork class, our teacher showed us a T-square. He said, "This is the most precious tool you will ever have and you must take care of it and never abuse it."

He left the class for a minute, so I took my T-square and pretended to beat it on my desk like a sledgehammer. I then felt this large, very large hand on my neck. He had found the class smartass and was going to kill me.

We then had a small gym for basketball, and I was very good at this as I had learned it at Sardis Elementary. (They had had a rough little outdoor court.) One day I got into a fight with another kid on the court. The principal asked the two of us to report to the gym at noon hour. He had two pairs of boxing gloves. He gave them to us and told us to put them on. He said, "You two are such smartasses, you have one hour to pummel each other." He wouldn't allow anyone else in but sat there and watched us for an hour. Many times we asked if we could stop. He would say, "Nope, you have forty minutes left." After the hour, we were absolutely exhausted. We could hardly stand up. I think we learned our lesson.

To the Garden of Eden

After junior high school, we went to Chilliwack Senior High, which had grades nine to thirteen. The last grade was called Senior Matric (senior matriculation) in those days. While in my first year, I carried on with my woodwork classes. And lo and behold, my teacher was a man named Laurence Peter, who was famed for his wild temper. One day while we class cut-ups, bored as usual, were stuffing sawdust in the ear of the class wimp, Peter was so enraged that he hurled a chisel at one kid and cut him over an eyebrow.

Years later, while working at the *Vancouver Sun*, I read a one-page piece in *Esquire* introducing to the world "The Peter Principle: everyone in any organization gets promoted one level above their level of competence." I ripped it out and pinned it on the *Sun* notice board where within minutes all of the reporters were laughing their heads off because it described, exactly, our newsroom. The *Sun* had taken the top reporter and made him city editor where he was a disaster. The former city editor was made the managing editor, even though he was completely incompetent.

I asked my researcher to find out who this genius Laurence Peter was. She came back three days later and said he was in charge of the University of Southern California's department studying handicapped children. She had traced his previous career from Western Washington College to the University of British Columbia to Chilliwack Senior High School. I almost fainted. This was my woodwork teacher. I tracked him down, we became good friends and dined together, and he told me he had devised his now-famous theory while at UBC when he discovered "that the reason academic politics were so vicious was because the stakes were so small."

In the Depression days, when of course there was no TV and no movies within miles of our home, my mother and her siblings had to make their own entertainment. So they taught themselves how to play the banjo and piano, and someone always had a trumpet or saxophone. When my mother had four children of her own, she insisted that we all learn to play a musical instrument. I had listened painfully for years to my two older sisters taking piano lessons: *Do-rey-me, do-rey-me.* When it came my turn, I said, "No way am I going near that [hated] piano."

"Well," my mother said, "you've got to play something."

I had seen an ad somewhere for guitar lessons. So I signed up for $45. On the day of my first lesson, my younger brother, Jack, and I were on the back of a flatbed truck, helping out as we often did the manager of the local feed store delivering sacks of whatever to the local farms. Jack and I never did get along, so we got into a fight and he pushed me off the truck. Unfortunately, it was travelling more than forty miles per hour, and I landed in the ditch with a broken wrist. That was the end of my musical career, and you must understand this is why Elvis Presley hit the charts because this obviously was years before he was invented.

To this day, I cannot play a note, sing a note, or blow a note. But, boy, can I dance. (Ask the girls.) I regret this inability to play an instrument when I go back to Saskatchewan and the Clarke family gets together for a good old-fashioned noisy romp. I do enjoy these evenings as much as I do going to my publishing buddy Kim McArthur's Christmas parties in Toronto where again every member of her family — grandparents, parents, and kids — play a musical instrument and we get together around the piano where her father, The Colonel, used to play sax as backup.

My first summer job was grafting roses in a nursery for 45 cents an hour. My next job was being a cherry picker, weekends and summers, for 5 cents a pound around the time there was a Chilliwack Annual Cherry Festival. I worked in a frozen food factory where my job was to spread peas over huge wire pads. I also worked in another frozen food place where we carried sides of beef off boxcars and there was practically one worker per week taken to hospital with a broken foot because a forty-pound salmon, frozen stiff, was like dropping a bowling ball on your pinkie. I worked in the Sardis post office during Christmas holidays licking stamps and sorting mail, and I now know the names of every small town in Saskatchewan and Manitoba where the mail was headed.

I also tried to get into the high wages of the logging industry and went to the Silver Skagit logging camp near Hope, British Columbia. I had to buy a pair of caulk logging boots, with special spikes in the soles, for $50. I was sixteen years old, and there was no training. I just showed up. On my second day I found myself, as "high loader," far up on a sixteen-wheel logging truck while a huge crane dropped swinging ten-foot-thick tree trunks so as not to crush me by coming down on my head. I lasted two days and didn't even make enough to pay for my boots. Besides, I was a coward. The B.C. logging industry has the highest number of fatalities per capita of any industry in Canada.

For the school paper I was writing a column called "High School Highlights." Les Barber, editor/owner of the weekly *Chilliwack Progress*, saw it and asked me to do a column for his paper. I took it down to him, and he later said he was astonished because he didn't have to change a single word. I was writing these things, of course, in longhand. Les paid me for a weekly column, and it suddenly occurred to me that I should learn to type.

In grade twelve I enrolled in a typing class, which was composed of thirty grade nine girls. I was the only boy, and the whole basketball team fell down laughing and ribbed me forever. So while the guitar lessons didn't work, the typing lessons certainly did. Obviously, I didn't know then that it would set me off in a career in journalism.

I wrote a column about a student experiment that involved feeding rats — in school corridor cages — Coke and junk food. We all know the resulting conclusions. A stiff-necked Coca-Cola lawyer threatened to sue for patent violation. (I was in high school, for Christ's sake!)

My major achievement was at the end of the year — the election of the boys' Senior Ring to head the student council. It was the "big swinging dick" of the school, and you had to have a B+ average. So my fellow jock friends couldn't go for it. They said I was a cinch. The day of the speech, which was outdoors on the grass, the whole school came out. At least half the school came by bus from a Mennonite community outside Chilliwack. Being Mennonite, they weren't allowed to stay after school, go to school dances, or turn out for sports. But they came to hear the speech.

At that time the trendy male thing was to have a streak of blond hair at the front, done with peroxide. I got up to give my speech with my peroxide streak, wearing green corduroy strides, which were twenty-six inches at the knee and six inches at the ankle. I had picked up a pair of saddle shoes in Vancouver and wore them. I got up in front of the Mennonites, looking like some stranger from space, and lost by four votes to Dave MacCaulay. Who went on to become superintendent of schools in Chilliwack. Dressed properly. Never got out of Chilliwack. Big mistake.

I didn't have enough money to go to university, so I took Senior Matric, which was the equivalent of grade thirteen. The fee was $112, which I didn't have to pay until after Christmas. I had no way of getting the $112 before then, so I figured I'd play basketball until Christmas and then quit.

Before that could happen, one day we noticed the principal standing with several men watching us as we changed classes. They hung around most of the day. I was doing the usual dumb things — punching the guys and goosing the girls as we walked down the halls. It turned out the men were from the National Film Board and were making a film called *Breakdown*. They were going to film it in Chilliwack, as a typical small Canadian town, and at Essondale, a mental hospital (as it was referred to in those days), which was fifty miles away.

They were looking for a typical young Canadian boy to play the younger brother to the professional actress playing the main part of someone having a nervous breakdown. So they called me in and said they had selected me, and I got the $112 for my final year in secondary school. University, here I come! Little did I know this brief encounter would be a precursor to my career.

The NFB paid me by the day, and it took several hours for shooting. At one stage I was to pull up to a gas station in a car. There was only one problem. I didn't know how to drive. My parents didn't have a car, and all of my buddies never stopped laughing because I was such a dolt in this regard. We had several runs at this shot because I only had to move the car about ten feet. I got it right for most of the shots except one. I let out the clutch too fast, and the car jumped in the air.

The "world premiere" of the film was at Chilliwack's only movie house and, of course, practically the whole school was there. And, of course, when it came to the shot at the gas station, they ran the one in which I goofed. The entire audience, including all my buddies, burst out laughing and continued for some five minutes.

3
Campus Chaff

While at high school I won both the 100-yard and 880-yard races. I didn't enter the 220 or the 440 because I was so lazy and had to develop stamina for those extended sprints. In the 880 I just trailed the field and then, because I was a sprinter, I made a mad dash the last fifty yards.

At the Fraser Valley annual track championships I won both the 100 and 880. I came home with two first-place red ribbons, but no one in my house paid any attention. I had to hitchhike from Chilliwack sixty-five miles to Vancouver to track meets, then hitchhike home. And through all of my many track meets, my parents never once attended. My mother was too busy running the Carman United Church choir, and my stepfather was the secretary-treasurer of the church — they being more interested in saving the natives in Africa. I resent that to this day.

Russ Dyer, our physical education teacher, arranged for me to get a track scholarship at the University of Washington in Seattle, which had a journalism school. An unfortunate visit to an illegal basketball tournament and a wrecked knee put an end to that. At Easter our basketball team was invited to a tournament in Trail, British Columbia, which pitted some of the best schools in British Columbia against some of the best in Alberta.

I approached Barry Harford, the principal, with the idea of participating. He was a wimp. I never did like him, and I don't think he liked me. He said, "Look, Allan, you took fourth, the highest outside-Vancouver school in the B.C. championships, and it was a great finish to the season. Why don't you quit while you're ahead?" The wrong thing to say to a stubborn seventeen-year-old. And he wouldn't give his permission.

Well, as captain, I figured, we would be on Easter holidays for ten days and no school could tell me what to do. One of the guys on the team, Bob Henderson, had a father who owned the town's only funeral home. We could get a hearse and could all pile into it one on top of the other. In those days there wasn't even a road from Chilliwack to Trail, which is almost in the Rocky Mountains. We had to drive down through the United States on a trip that almost took a day.

On the second day of the tournament, after I scored fourteen points in the first half of a game and was headed for the highest total I'd ever had, I wrecked my knee and spent the rest of the tournament hobbling around on crutches. We then had to take the day-long trip back home and piled on top of one another again, which didn't do the untreated knee any good. So it was almost a week before I finally got to a doctor, who put the entire leg into a cast.

Some months later, the day I was to have the cast cut off, the team played a noon-hour softball game against the teachers to raise money for my doctor's bills. I walked back to the school from the doctor's office, and grateful for what they were doing, I offered to go up to bat and hit some fly balls before the game. *Stupid.* I took one swing — *crunch!* There went the knee again. Typical show-off. The principal shook his head — the "I told you so" reaction.

With my leg up I managed to get through Senior Matric. A chap called Owen Nelmes (who later became my brother-in-law) went to orientation at the University of British Columbia and saw on the notice board something called "University Co-operative Society." It was a house run by a revolving group of students — twelve in all — and presided over by a fat English lady who cooked and cleaned. You paid your monthly rent until graduation to be replaced by another flood of freshmen. Owen was a year ahead of me at Chilliwack and had gone to the University of Washington, hoping to get into medical school. Once there he realized he would never be able to afford it and returned to pharmacy school at UBC. The two of us wound up at the co-op.

Teachers at Chilliwack Senior High had been urging me to go to university because they could see that I could write. The UBC campus newspaper, *The Ubyssey* (the UBC initials being a bad play on *The Odyssey*), was famous for turning out people such as Pierre Berton, Eric Nicol, Lister Sinclair, and dozens of other top Canadian journalists. On the first day of university I went down to the paper's office in the basement of Brock Hall and was sent out on an assignment. I had never been told before what to write. The next day I went in again and was sent out on another assignment. After writing it and handing it in, I said to myself: *To hell with this.*

I went home to the co-op, sat down, and wrote in longhand a column attacking the UBC engineers as a bunch of weaklings and morons who couldn't even attract a girlfriend.

I went to *The Ubyssey* office and threw the article into the basket on the desk. The following day I picked up the paper, and my column was on the front page where it stayed for my short three years at *The Ubyssey*.

My knee having now recovered, I tried out for the junior varsity basketball squad, the JVs. One afternoon, after practice, I was walking out of the gym when a gang of husky engineering students, led by Paul White, grabbed me, threw me into a car, and drove me downtown. The number one meeting place and the busiest intersection in Vancouver was at Granville and Georgia in front of the Birks Jewellers clock. The engineers chained me to the towering clock and locked me in with large padlocks, then fled. Everybody in Vancouver coming out of work at 5:00 p.m. looked at me as if I were nuts. Somebody finally phoned the fire station, and some firemen came and cut me loose with bolt cutters.

With my brother, Jack, at my high school graduation in 1950. That's me on the left. How did I afford that suit?

Boy from Nowhere

So my column, which was called "Campus Chaff," stepped up the attacks on the engineers. When *The Ubyssey* had its term end, it had a dinner at a restaurant in Stanley Park where I took Pat Arnold, my girl-friend. Just as the dinner was beginning, a waiter came over and said someone was at the door asking for me. I went to the door, and guess what. Four more engineer thugs grabbed me and put me into a car. One of them walked in, sat in the chair beside Miss Arnold, and said I wouldn't be back that evening. The engineers then drove me across Lions Gate Bridge to West Vancouver way up in the forest, took what little money I had, and left me in the darkness, miles from anywhere. I had to walk and walk and walk. Finally, I found a farmhouse and had to tell the rather dubious occupants what had happened. They lent me enough money to take a taxi home.

The engineers were famous for their annual three-day drunk, which their graduating class had at the Commodore Ballroom in downtown Vancouver. The Commodore was the most well-known party place in town. I had waited three years for my revenge. We followed the president of the class to a Safeway parking lot, grabbed him, and drove seventy miles

The Ubyssey float during a protest parade. I'm the editor, standing at the back with the cool coat on.

to Cultus Lake where we had rented a cabin. Sitting there with him for three days, we published huge headlines in *The Ubyssey* announcing that the president had mysteriously disappeared and hadn't shown up to what was to be the culmination of his university career.

When I was playing for the UBC Thunderbirds junior varsity basketball team, our games were broadcast because we played in the Vancouver Senior League against the Vancouver Clover Leafs, the Canadian champions. On my team were Robin Abercrombie, John Shippobotham, and Allan Fotheringham. There were three nervous breakdowns among the radio broadcasters when they tried to follow the play and would say, "Fotheringham passed to Shippobotham who passes to Abercrombie to …" by which time the other team had scored twice.

In the first half of our first game of the season against the famous Clover Leafs, I leaped up to intercept a pass. When I came down, the knee was gone once again. This time I had to have an operation, so I went to Dean Gage, the head of the arts faculty, and asked for a student loan to pay for the medical costs of $135.

At the time I was paying my way through university by going down to the *Vancouver Sun* at nights and writing up UBC sports. To get there, it was a long bus ride from the university and I had to change buses. There was a wait of about fifteen minutes at the changeover, and unfortunately the bus sat idling in front of a men's clothing store. Back then the fashion among all the swish fraternity lads was a tweed topcoat. Stark in the window of the men's shop was a beautiful grey topcoat. I had to sit and look at it every night for weeks. Temptation is a terrible thing. Of course, the day I walked into the administration office at UBC to sign the necessary forms for the student loan, the first person to stroll in the door was Dean Gage, who immediately looked at this impoverished little boy who had no money but was wearing a beautiful grey tweed topcoat.

During my university years, my main girlfriend was Helen (Donnelly) Hutchinson, who worked on the paper and later achieved fame as a national host of CBC Radio's *Morningside* show before Peter Gzowski. At UBC parties — she had a wit as sharp as a tack — people would almost pay admission to come to such parties to listen to Helen and me insult each other. We had some silly little spat, and I didn't phone her for a week. At the time the sorority girls decided to have a crazy football game and enlisted Jack Hutchinson of the B.C. Lions to teach them the rules and coach them. Helen was the quarterback. By the time I had decided to repair the spat, she had so wowed Jack that she later married him. That was the first of her three marriages. She now lives around the corner from my wife and me in Toronto.

With time, in 1953, I became the editor of *The Ubyssey*. Joe Schlesinger was the previous editor. Joe, who went on to achieve fame as a highly respected correspondent around the world for the CBC, sat in his office and never spoke to me for the entire term, being noted as a silent recent refugee from Czechoslovakia. He approached me one day and asked if I was going to put my name forward for his position.

I was the sports editor at the time. I said I hadn't thought of it as there was another person, Ed Parker, who seemed to be a shoo-in because he had been waiting for years for the spot and was also sleeping with the news editor. Joe urged me to enter my name. So I did and won the vote twelve to two. Parker and his girlfriend being the two. There were rumours that Joe had stuffed the ballot box, he being a Czech from afar who knew how to do such things. In our meetings in our foreign correspondent days in Paris or London or wherever, when the wine started to flow I would tell that story. Joe would neither confirm nor deny but state, "Yes, and Fotheringham is still writing the same sports stories, just changing the names." However, he has always enjoyed the speculation.

The tradition at *The Ubyssey* was to make the final paper of the year the "Goon Edition." That year we decided to spoof the three downtown papers. And since some of us were working part-time at those papers, we stole the typefaces from the composing rooms and renamed the *Vancouver Sun*, "The Vancouver Fun," Vancouver's *Province* became the "Vancouver Providence," and the *News Herald* became the "Few Herald." The *Sun* was owned by the two Cromie brothers. We called them the "Crummie" brothers. Columnist Mamie Maloney became Mamie "Baloney." Sports editor Erwin Swangard, who I, of course, worked for in the sports department, we called, "Squirming S. Vanguard."

The UBC Thunderbird rugby team was playing its final game of the season against the University of California Golden Bears. I was high in the UBC press box when I suddenly saw the hulking figure of Erwin Swangard climbing the steps. There was no place for me to run. "Okay, kit," he said in his heavy German accent, "I'm gonna sue you, I am gonna sue da Alma Mater Society, and I am gonna sue da university."

My university graduation photograph. I was one of the few Ubyssey *editors to actually graduate.*

Boy from Nowhere

My life flashed before my eyes. I was about to take final exams, having not attended classes for the year I was editor. I was $400 in debt for another student loan and money my sister, Donna, had loaned me for university. Now I would have no job.

Several days later it grew worse. I received a very official letter under the letterhead of Don Cromie, the *Vancouver Sun* publisher. It said in very legal language that *The Ubyssey* had defiled and libelled in a vicious manner his paper and demanded to know the identity of the person responsible for this. I just about fainted until I got to the P.S., which said that such a person obviously had some talent in his viciousness and would he be interested in a position near the executive leather top chairs. I didn't know if this was a joke or whether he was serious. So I went down to see Don, a man I had never met before. He spent the entire interview with his feet on his desk while trying to flip paper clips over the overhead lamp. I got the job.

Campus Chaff

THE VANCOUVER SUN

OFFICE OF THE PUBLISHER

Monday
April 5
1 9 5 4

Editor
Ubyssey
University of British Columbia
VANCOUVER, B.C.

Dear Sir:

It has been drawn to my attention that
a purported newspaper titled The Vancouver Son,
imitating the type and hed style and satirizing
some of The Sun's general styles and manners,
has been published, allegedly by The Ubyssey.
This satirical publication libels, ridicules and
generally damages The Sun to a grievous degree,
with malice aforethought. It also applies a lesser
amount of its pages to similar malicious mimicry of
two other local newspapers.

After legal advice, it would be appreciated
if the writer could be informed of the identity of
author and editor of this work, and advised also
whether said Perpetrator might be interested in a
Salaried Position at The Sun.(see footnote)

Yours truly,

PUBLISHER

We might refuse to break our editorial rule of starting
newcomers above $1000 a month, but despite our editorial
condition of already being well staffed by highly skilled
"position foot-workers", a person of the skill and ruth-
lessness of the above mentioned Perpetrator should have no
misgivings about advancement once installed, as offered
above, within knife's reach of the morocco covered swivel
chairs, previous frightening although temporary experiences
notwithstanding.

4
To Warsaw on a Scooter

The day Don Cromie hired me I was sent to see the managing editor, Hal Straight, a frightening monster of a man of some 260 pounds. He and the now-famous Pierre Berton put out the morning edition by 10:00 a.m. and then drove to the bushes of Stanley Park and drank a twenty-six-ouncer of rye from the neck of the bottle, came back, and put out the afternoon edition. Berton being the star reporter.

As I walked into Straight's office, I vowed I would demand $50 a week. Stupidly, I asked, "Am I worth $50 a week?"

The managing editor said, "At the moment you are not worth a god-damn cent. Forty-five dollars a week — seven o'clock Monday morning. See you."

Straight sent me to work for Erwin Swangard, who for the first six months wouldn't talk to me. Every Monday morning at the sports section meeting he turned to Merv Peters, his assistant editor, and said, "Tell Fotheringham to cover the lacrosse game in New Westminster."

Peters, who was sitting about four feet away from Swangard, then turned to me and said, "Fotheringham, cover the lacrosse game in New Westminster." He resented me because I was the only one with a university degree in the department, so he added, "Take the company car. You can drive, of course?"

I said, "Of course."

But, of course, I couldn't. (Remember that Chilliwack movie?) I still didn't have a driver's licence, so I asked my sister, Irene, who was in nursing school in Vancouver, to come with me for support.

In those days streetcar tracks ran from Vancouver fifteen miles to New Westminster. I shifted the car into second gear, put the wheels in the streetcar tracks, and drove at twenty miles an hour to my destination. My sister was so frightened that she took the bus home. I drove the company car all summer on assignments and learned to drive. Three months later I took the driver's licence test. That was another form of learning on the job.

Years later I was in Palm Springs, California, speaking to the Canadian-American Friendship Society. I walked into the hotel, and there was Don Cromie, by now of course long retired in his winter retreat. The society had asked him to introduce me, and he told a story I had never heard.

Six months after he hired me he called Erwin Swangard in and asked, "Whatever happened to that kid from UBC that we hired?"

Swangard said, "Well, he's lazy, he's a troublemaker, he won't take orders from anybody, and he's always late for work."

"Well, get rid of him," Cromie said. "Don't keep him around just because I hired him."

"Oh, no," Swangard said. "He's the brightest guy in the whole newsroom and has a tremendous future in journalism."

As a sportswriter, I covered lacrosse, hockey, and football. One person I met while covering football was a young guy named Bobby Ackles. He was the water boy for the B.C. Lions. Bobby worked his way up the ranks — equipment manager, et cetera. He then somehow was hired by the Dallas Cowboys as a scout. Bobby advanced through the National Football League ranks and eventually became a coach with the Las Vegas franchise.

The smart guy who owned the Lions, now Senator David Braley, brought him back to Vancouver and made him president where he used to carry the water buckets.

I put Bobby in touch with a ghost writer and a publisher to tell his amazing life story, which was published in 2007. He then had a boat called *The Water Buoy*, also the title of his book. Sadly, in 2008, he died of a heart attack on the dock at Bowen Island while walking back to his boat with his morning coffee.

At the last birthday bash for me that Bobby attended on Bowen Island in 2006 he and his wife, Kay, brought me a B.C. Lions jersey with my name and the year of my birth on the back. It is something I will remember him by and cherish.

When I graduated from UBC in 1954, I was appalled at the low wages journalists were paid, so I made a deal with myself. I vowed to stay in the business for three years, and if I didn't reach a certain level of advancement, I'd quit and go to law school. I was within six months of the self-imposed deadline and thought I was destined to be a lawyer. Then two things happened.

Like all sportswriters, I worked at night, covering a hockey game, a football game, whatever, then came back to the office to write the story and, of course, ended up in Chinatown past midnight with the boys telling one another lies and gossip. Such a lifestyle meant I woke up at about noon and had all afternoon free. One afternoon I was at Kitsilano Beach, looking for girls as usual, when I ran into Bill Popowich, who I had graduated with at UBC where he was captain of the university soccer team.

Bill had just returned from Europe, and he changed my life when he told me his tales of youth hostels, London, Paris, Rome, and all the other delights. I wondered what I was doing sitting on Kitsilano Beach, and at that moment I decided to travel to Europe as soon as I had enough money.

Shortly thereafter there was a shuffle at the newspaper and I was offered the job of sports editor. I was only twenty-four, and that was the most unusual promotion. So I knew I could make it in the business and immediately quit and went to Europe to bum around for three years. Everyone in the building thought I was nuts. It was 1957.

I went to New York, saw Mickey Mantle play at Yankee Stadium, and took the Holland-America liner *Statendam* to Southampton. Onboard I met two girls who had just graduated from Vassar, the female Ivy League school. They were going on the usual grand tour of Europe and had picked out all of their hotels and restaurants in London, Paris, and Madrid. They were great fun, and when we got to London, they persuaded me to go to these fancy restaurants with them.

Me, who had saved $1,500 and was going to do Europe living in youth hostels.

One night we were in a Greek restaurant in Soho and suddenly there was a huge crush of men walking in, guarding a couple. It was Prince and Princess Michael of Kent, and I realized I was in the wrong league and told the girls goodbye.

I then took a ferry across the English Channel to begin my great adventure and bunked into a youth hostel at Dieppe. Wandering down the beach, I saw a nice little restaurant and went in to have a beautiful steak that I discovered to my amazement was very rare and bloody. It was the first time I ever knew there was blood in meat, having come from Hearne, Saskatchewan, where all meat was done to the texture of a boot.

The suitcase I was going to use for six months was so heavy that I had to take a taxi out of town to get to a highway to hitchhike. Reaching Holland, I was picked up by a magician going to a magicians' convention. He got a flat tire, and I helped him change the tire. Some miles down the road I realized that my glasses had fallen into the ditch. So I had to hitch-hike the opposite way and figure out where, in a country that had four million identical ditches, my glasses might be.

I was down on my hands and knees when a car stopped and the driver asked, "What are you doing?" I explained, and he said I would never find the glasses and to get in his car. I told him my great plan to conquer Europe by foot and he said, "Come with me." Then he took me to his home, and it turned out he was a Vespa dealer. The dream answer to my unplanned life.

It took three days to get a two-wheeled Vespa shipped in. Because it was late in the afternoon and I wanted to get to Hamburg that night, the Vespa dealer offered to give me a lesson on the scooter. In my hurry to get out of town, I said, "No, don't worry." (This, of course, was in the days of no helmets being worn.)

I got about a half-mile out of town when a huge truck went by. With a blast of air, the next thing I knew, I woke up in the ditch with the Vespa on top of me. I looked up and saw four huge wooden shoes occupied by two farmers, who pulled me out.

Rain or shine, through Denmark, Sweden, and East Germany on the way to Warsaw, I had to exist with just my sunglasses. When I made it to Stockholm, I stayed with Dr. Lusztig, the Hungarian father of Peter Lusztig, my university roommate in Vancouver. I was preparing to leave Stockholm to drive back through Denmark and then into West Germany to make my way to Berlin. He told me there was a ferry from the tip of Sweden to East Germany, which would cut miles and countries off my itinerary.

I landed in East Germany with no papers or relevant documents. The authorities, after much puzzlement, gave me a one-day pass, saying I had to go straight to Berlin without stopping to get there that night.

Under a heavy rain, I was frightened to death and was speeding as fast as I could when the road suddenly changed into cobblestones. The Vespa and I parted company once more. I was just outside a farm, and the farmer hauled me into the barn while the cows stared at me strangely and mooed as he hammered the damaged scooter into operation.

This took so long that there was no way I could reach Berlin as ordered that day. So I stopped at a small inn, went downstairs for dinner, and to my horror saw three East German policemen in their ominous uniforms. The chef came over and handed me a menu which, of course, I couldn't understand, so I just pointed at three different items.

"*Nein,*" he said, becoming quite agitated. And I, not wanting to cause any attention, insisted on what I had ordered. He kept shouting at me. By this time, everyone in the restaurant was gazing my way.

I understood why when he finally returned with the three items I had ordered. Baked potato, fried potatoes, and boiled potatoes. And I, knowing everyone was gawking at me, ate them all down happily as if I did that every day. The three policemen, laughing, sent over a quart of beer. Trying to escape being jailed, I sent them back three quarts. They sent me back another quart. It was a very long evening.

Because I had arranged while at the *Vancouver Sun* to meet a copy girl named Helena Zukowski in Warsaw at high noon on July 1, I was in a panic. She had won a scholarship to study in Poland because of her Polish heritage, and I had figured there would be a main railway station in Warsaw and obviously there would be a big clock there. Of course, that was months before I left Vancouver. I had said I would stand below the clock at high noon on July 1.

Setting out through East Germany to Berlin, I immediately found a youth hostel. I then wandered around and came upon a food fair and saw they had a money exchange. I had arranged a visa for Poland in London, and the travel agency had exchanged the money for me, enough for my two weeks in Warsaw.

The exchange rate was one grosz to the dollar and a hundred groszy to one złoty. In the Berlin exchange I found it was four groszy to the dollar. So I was suddenly rich.

After several days, I headed for the Polish border again without proper papers or visa. They were so puzzled again by this silly kid on a Vespa that they somehow let me through. On the first day in Poland I was speeding toward Poznań. The Polish rural roads were filled with chickens, pigs, cows, everything.

Late in the afternoon I came across a herd of cows crossing the road. I stopped and let all of them go by except one lonely cow trailing the herd. When I zoomed the Vespa, the cow suddenly turned around and came back across the road.

I went ass over teakettle across the cow and landed on the rough macadam road with its raised gravel. It removed two layers of skin from each of my ten fingers. There are only two levers on a Vespa on the handlebars. One is the gas and the other is the brake. So each time I squeezed one of them, blood oozed out of my fingertips.

It was 5:00 p.m. when I arrived in Poznań. Everybody was leaving their offices and lining up at the bus stop. They looked at me, this guy with sunglasses, no helmet, and a wild red beard with blood dripping from his fingertips. A man stepped out of the lineup and said, "Come with me," and took me down an alley.

I didn't know if he was planning on mugging me or raping me. He produced a key and guided me through the back door. It turned out he was a pharmacist. Taking me into his store, he bandaged me up.

Still trying to get to Warsaw by July 1 to meet Helena, I left Poznań early the next morning. After dropping my bags off at the Windsor Hotel in Warsaw, I went to the clock at the railway station and stood there for

At play during my European travels.

45

Boy from Nowhere

four hours. She never showed up. The next time I saw her, years later, she was editor of a magazine in Palm Springs, California. She apologized.

Upon returning to the hotel, my good fortune due to the exchange rate was immediately apparent to the staff. Because I had this ridiculous money that I had bought for 25 percent of its worth, I couldn't bother with all of these hundreds of groszy that were tearing holes in my trousers. So I dumped them in a wastepaper basket in my hotel room.

The word soon got around through the cleaning women that a mad American millionaire was so rich he was throwing away money. Probably a week's wages for them. So whenever I went down to the hotel dining room, three or four waiters attempted to elbow one another's teeth out in order to serve me and get the tip.

Shortly after arriving, I sent a dispatch to the *Vancouver Sun*, which it ran on the front page. In the piece I said, in my innocence, "The secret police cannot be seen anywhere in Warsaw." My close friend, Carol Gregory from *The Ubyssey* days, read this and sent a letter to the editor, stating that she wasn't aware that people walked around Warsaw with badges on their jacket saying, "Hey, I am the secret police."

As arranged in London, I had to have a Polish government tourist guide, and the young lady showed me all over town. By this time, I was fed up with the sunglasses and explained to her that I wanted to cut short the visit to get back to Berlin so I could buy new glasses. She sympathized with my plight and arranged for me to leave. So I left the whole country by making a profit.

Upon returning to Berlin, I met at the youth hostel a young South African architect who was doing the same thing as I was on a motorcycle. Someone who could come in very useful when years later I went to Cape Town to release Nelson Mandela from jail. We roamed around Germany together and then down to Austria. One day in Vienna, in heavy traffic, he was ahead of me and jumped the red light. I had to stop. As a result, we lost each other.

When I finally got back to London, I walked into a flat to pick up a girlfriend, and there was my old South African buddy in the same room, taking another girl out. Small world.

Then I went to Venice, Rome, over to Monaco, and the rest of France on the way to Spain where I was going to spend the winter and write the great

Canadian novel. I found a little inn outside Málaga owned by a Dutchman who couldn't speak English. One night he came to me, pointed at the sky, and started to bark. I couldn't figure out why he was barking until he got through to me that the Soviets had just launched *Sputnik* with a dog in it.

The great Canadian novel not complete, I headed north for London. I came out of sleepy Spain into the first French town where it was filled with crazy French drivers. A guy zoomed out of a side street and hit me. I went up in the air and came down on top of the scooter.

Luckily, I didn't come down in front of it as I would have been killed. I woke up in the hospital, not being able to speak a word of French. None of the staff in this small town in this small hospital could speak English. They had seized my wallet and my passport while trying to figure out what to do with me.

One day a man walked into my room. He said in English, "I fought with Canadian troops in Korea and they were good guys. I saw the picture of your wrecked scooter on the front page of the paper. What can I do for you?"

His name was Guy Chaumont. He had been an officer in the French Army and had just won the Legion of Honour (the French version of our Victoria Cross). Guy explained that because of this honour he had the authority to deal with all sorts of officials and solve my problems. He got my scooter fixed, bullied the hospital authorities so I didn't have to pay, and took me home to recuperate with his wife, who was an American.

When I got to Paris, I stayed with a couple of girls from Vancouver — Carol Gregory and a friend. I was down to $10 and went to American Express to get it changed. As I walked along, a guy kept following me and whispered, "Money change, money change." These wide boys, of course, hung around American Express, since they knew that was where the dumb tourists were going to be.

At that time, as in Poland, French currency was at an artificial rate, and this guy was offering me a much better deal. He said, "Follow me." We walked and walked through alleys and around corners and came to a deserted building. He arranged a deal, and I tried to offer him my money, but the guy said, "No, no. Wait here."

He went away for five to ten minutes, then returned with a big thick envelope that looked to be about the right size for the money I was to receive. After he handed it to me, I gave him my money, then he turned and ran off. I opened my envelope, and it was filled with newsprint. I sat on the curb and cried.

A policeman came along and asked what was the matter. I explained. He shook his head, shrugged, and walked away. Another dumb tourist fleeced outside American Express. I borrowed enough money off Carol to get me across the channel to England and arrived at the home of old friends Patricia and Tony Prosser with one cup of gas left in the Vespa.

5
London Town

I couldn't get a journalism job in London but heard they were always short of substitute teachers in the east end of the city. The east end was slums. Full of poverty and crime.

Going out there, I found that the teachers gathered down the street some distance from the school and walked in together for safety. Apparently, if you went in alone across the schoolyard, the kids supposedly playing pickup soccer would aim the ball at you, occasionally accompanying it with rocks.

I was shifted around from class to class. One day in the teachers' room, completely confused, I asked where I had to go for my next class. A gnarled old senior teacher said to me, "Stay here, man. This is the safest room we've got." The school had wire mesh on all the windows to protect everyone from the rocks and debris the kids hurled. I wasn't a success as a substitute teacher.

Then I discovered there was a small paper on Fleet Street called *Canada News*. It was owned by Roy Thomson's empire and was put out for the benefit of the Canadian troops on bases in Germany. So cheap was the operation that it relied on dupes of Canadian Press copy mailed over from Canada.

We would edit the copy and ship it up to the paper in Edinburgh, which Thomson owned. It was printed there, sent back, and then dispatched to Germany. This process took so long that the troops got the Grey Cup results just about when the baseball season opened.

Three women worked in the office. They told me that the previous editor, who was from Victoria, was a very morose man, as anyone working on Thomson wages would be. One Monday morning he didn't appear at work. Tuesday he didn't show up. Wednesday he didn't show up. By this time, they detected a funny smell coming from an unused closet at the back of the office.

They opened the door and found the man, who had hanged himself. I always waited in glee for the first time I ever ran into Ken Thomson, son of Lord Thomson, and I would say, "Oh, Mr. Thomson, we have a mutual family friend."

I never thought that years later I would meet at Rosedale cocktail parties a now-aging Ken Thomson who, in fact, inherited his father's peerage but never once went to the House of Lords and declined to use the title that was his. He told me he was a great fan of my column, which appeared in the *Globe and Mail*, one of his papers.

Eventually, I found myself living in a basement flat with five Australians. One was an architect, another was an engineer named Vaughan Dobbins, a third was journalist Dick Conigrave, and the others were always out of work. It was a terrible place when in the winter the wallpaper was soaked in water.

The first Saturday night I was there, as the lads prepared to head out to the pub, the first one took a bath in the only tub. When he got out, he yelled, "Next!" To my astonishment, the next Aussie climbed into the same water. When he got out, a third guy got in. That was how much hot water the flat had.

Some months later Elliott Leyton, a friend from Vancouver, arrived in need of a free bed. When Saturday night arrived, I casually climbed into filthy, cooling water and beckoned him to follow. He glared at me as if I had lost my mind, and I realized I had adapted to the circumstances.

Elliott is now a professor at Memorial University in Newfoundland, is a world-renowned expert on serial killers, and is quoted in newspapers around the globe.

Aussies are a different breed. It's a known historical fact that Britain, attempting to populate the far-off island colony, sent English convicts to settle in Australia. So, after a few pints at week's end in the local pub, I used to say to the Aussie blokes, "You guys come from the worst criminals in England."

The Aussies replied, "No, every one of our ancestors were individually chosen by the finest judges of England!"

One of their rituals was that every Sunday they would open the fridge, collect the leftovers, chop them up, and whip them with eggs. The result was what we called a "meadow muffin," which went down well with beer. Decades later I made the same thing for my children and their spouses. They sat there politely and ate the disgusting dish that I was so proud of.

In time I got a job on the North American desk at Reuters in the most prestigious building on Fleet Street. There were six of us, and our total job was to take the wire copy coming in from around the world and change the word *lorry* to the word *truck* and the word *bonnet* (on a car) to *hood*, which is what it was called across the ocean. The work wasn't exactly mind-expanding.

All of this was in the 1950s when every home in London burned coal as fuel. When the word *smog* was invented by *Time*, meaning smoke mixed with fog. In the winter in London it got so bad that elderly people with lung problems died by the score. The Reuters newsroom was fifty yards long, and sometimes at night we couldn't see the other end of the place.

One night I was doing a rewrite about Prince Charles and yelled over my shoulder, "How old is Charles?"

I heard this voice from an American whose name was Ed Fitzgerald, who said, "He was born at 9:14 p.m. on Sunday, November 14, 1948."

We scraped together enough money to get tuxedo rentals for Vaughan Dobbins's London marriage in 1958. That's me in the foreground on the far left.

"How do you know that?" I asked.

"I'll tell you a little story. I was bureau chief at United Press International in London. As you can imagine, with the birth of a future king imminent, there was a ferocious race between the different wire services to get the news first to all of the papers in the United States.

"So I came up with a brilliant plan. We would write, waiting for the birth, two stories. One would say, 'Queen Elizabeth tonight gave birth to a boy.' Followed by all of the attended drivel. The second story would say, 'Queen Elizabeth gave birth to a girl.' With all of the usual details of what that would mean in the royal line.

"We had an attendant, the usual dumb Englishman who transmitted the copy to New York. There were two keys that sat before him. All he had to do when we got the word from the attendant we had standing outside Buckingham Palace was to push either the boy key or the girl key.

"One of his buddies, on his coffee break, came over to gossip with him and rested his elbow over — guess what? The girl key that went off to New York and three hundred newspapers. That's why I'm no longer bureau chief of United Press International."

Because of the Australians, I met at a party one night a seventeen-year-old girl called Leonie Leahy, whom one of the guys had met on the ship from Australia to England. She was a dancer and immediately got a job in the chorus of *My Fair Lady*, the biggest musical ever to hit London.

The original stage-door Johnnie, I waited at the outside theatre door after seeing *My Fair Lady* thirty-seven times and took her home on the back seat of my Vespa. She was the second strongest Catholic in the world after the pope.

We went to cast parties where I met Rex Harrison and his lady, Kay Kendall, who tragically died young of cancer. Leonie ended up as the prima ballerina of the Oslo State Opera in Norway.

One day at a party where all of the Canadians and the Aussies got into the brown ale, Jerry Lecovin, a guy I'd gone to UBC with, arrived. He was a lawyer I'd never met personally but had seen many times in the student reviews where he did a great imitation of Groucho Marx. Jerry explained at the party that he had this great idea to buy a Volkswagen and go through Russia, this being 1959 when the Soviets allowed foreign tourists to bring their own vehicles into the country.

He needed two other guys to share the cost with him to make it viable. "Fotheringham," Jerry said, "you know everybody. Find me two other guys."

I quickly found Keith Powers, a crazy Canadian journalist from Thunder Bay. And they urged me to become the third. I said I couldn't possibly because I'd been saving for three years to get back to Vancouver to get a real job.

Months went by and one morning, after Powers finished the all-night shift at Reuters, we met with Lecovin in a greasy spoon for breakfast. Lecovin said he was abandoning the idea because he couldn't come up with a third person.

I sat there and suddenly thought to myself, *I'm going back to Canada, and for the rest of my life whenever the words* Soviet Union *come up in the conversation, I'll be saying, "Oh, I could have gone there once, you know."*

Common sense sank in and I said, "I'm a go."

At the Finland–Soviet Union border we were all lined up in the customs shed with a pack of American businessmen. Off in the corner was a gang of large, fat, old Russian women, all dressed black to their ankles — and one beautiful young blonde.

They were the official Soviet Intourist guides who had to accompany each group. "Mr. Weinstein of Detroit," an official called out, and he was assigned one of the oldies. It went on and on, the oldies gradually disappearing.

Powers, Lecovin, and I stood in wild anticipation. Surely, surely, we wouldn't have the luck to get the blonde. Finally, the last fat old lady was dispatched and we were introduced to twenty-five-year-old Ella Dimitrieva, who would be our companion in the tiny Volkswagen for three whole weeks on the way to the Black Sea.

Lecovin's plan was to get to Istanbul, turn left, and head back to Vancouver across India and Burma, while Powers and I would get back to our jobs in London on my Vespa scooter, which I had shipped from Copenhagen to Athens.

Ella as an eight-year-old child had been through the siege of Leningrad and had been so weak she couldn't get out of bed, her sole ration being one raw potato. The streets were so clogged with corpses that the survivors were too weak to carry them away. As we drove to Moscow, Karkhov, and Kiev, we took her dancing at night in the best hotels. She suddenly discovered lipstick and somehow acquired silk stockings.

Alas, all was not well with Lecovin. The guy I'd seen so funny on the stage at UBC turned out to be mean, a cheapskate who tried to cheat farmers when they sold us gas. He was completely humourless in person, which was tough when you were three weeks in a Volkswagen with four people.

The original plan was to drive through Romania and Bulgaria on the way to Istanbul. But the famed Soviet bureaucracy came into play. They gave us a visa to Bulgaria, but not to Romania. We couldn't get to Bulgaria without crossing Romania. So we had to take a ship from Kiev to Odessa on the Black Sea.

First they told us there was no road between the large city of Kiev and the large city of Odessa, which was laughable, of course. When we laughed at them, they then said we couldn't drive ourselves because of military reasons and they would supply us with a driver while we took the train there. We laughed that one off. I should add here that Powers and I had this brilliant idea of paying for the trip by taking pictures of every pretty Russian girl we saw and selling them to *Playboy* as a "Girls Of Russia" feature.

The final night in Odessa, overlooking the sea from a beautiful restaurant, we had dinner and fond words for Ella. Much wine, much laughs, and she took us down to the dock, kissed us all goodbye, and then turned us over to the police, who seized all of our photographs.

Lecovin, while Powers and I were dallying with Ella, had gone in first, and they had seized his camera. Instead of coming back and warning us, he scuttled aboard the ship to save himself. Powers and I insisted we weren't going to budge until we got our cameras back.

At first they claimed they had a photo lab and would process the pictures there. Stubbornly, we waited, knowing that was nonsense, and then they admitted it wasn't true but they were keeping the cameras. We said we weren't getting on the ship until we got our cameras back. They then came to us and said the ship was leaving at 6:00 a.m. and if we didn't board we would be in Russia with an expired visa.

We got onboard and didn't speak to Lecovin, who had betrayed us for his own safety, for the three days it took the ship to stop in Romania and Bulgaria before reaching Istanbul. In Istanbul Lecovin turned left and we turned right. Powers and I picked up my Vespa in Athens and went back to London.

After returning to Vancouver, I wrote about the experience in my column, naming names. Lecovin avoided me for years.

Upon my return to London, I worked for a while at Reuters. But since I had used up all of the money intended for my flight to Vancouver on the trip to Russia and knowing it was time to return to Canada, my parents sent me cash for the airfare home.

6
Newspaper Madness

A dignified and shy girl arrives from England to be Erwin Swangard's new secretary. On her first day veteran reporter Barry Broadfoot walks by her desk, puts down a dime, and walks on. He does the same thing every day until two weeks later the bewildered Ann Barling summons up the courage to ask him what he's doing.

"When it gets to forty bucks," explains Broadfoot, "I want a piece of tail."

This was the *Vancouver Sun* of the 1950s.

At the office Christmas party Nelles Hamilton and Don Stainsby get into a fistfight. Somebody always got into a fight at the office Christmas party. No one paid any attention to them until we heard a blood-curdling scream. Nelles had Stainsby pinioned across an office desk, which as usual was two feet deep in stale newspapers, yellowing copy paper, and dead cheese sandwiches — all disguising that Stainsby was impaled through his back by a buried copy spike.

This was the *Vancouver Sun* of the 1950s.

When *Sputnik* went up, publisher Don Cromie ordered *Sun* photogs to the top of Cromie-owned Grouse Mountain across the harbour on the theory that the *Sun*, being five thousand feet closer to a world scoop, would catch the satellite as it flew past. Deni Eagland — or was it Brian Kent? — drew a sharp fingernail across a negative and (presto!) we had another international first.

At the famous Cromie annual blowout at the Commodore Ballroom, after Don unveiled a huge red neon sign signifying a record two hundred thousand circulation and rolled out onstage a white Cadillac convertible for the circulation manager, Bobby Ackles — originally, the water boy of the B.C. Lions, later general manager, and still later a high poobah with the Dallas Cowboys — punched out assistant sports editor Merv Peters all the way down the Commodore's celebrated long staircases.

We separated them, made them shake hands, and went off to fetch the car. By the time we got back, Ackles had knocked out Merv's lights and kicked him in a knee, which required serious hospital time. Ah, fun times.

Tom Thumb Butler was quietly typing in the sports room when the cops walked in. They wanted him in the slammer immediately for forty-three unpaid parking tickets. We had to do a whip-around to save him from a criminal record.

Stu McNeill, who was the Canadian Army hundred-yard sprint champion in Europe during the war, was the natural expert to cover the 1954 four-minute mile showdown between Roger Bannister and John Landy at Vancouver's British Empire Games.

A week before the event, emboldened by the grape, Stu was detected outside the Kerrisdale Arena after covering a lacrosse game, waving in taxis and offering $20 bills to anyone who would accept his largesse. Erwin busted him to covering archery and badminton for the Games, giving the priceless track assignment to me, a kid who had just graduated months earlier from UBC.

The next night Stu warmed up — awaiting Erwin's arrival — by hurling typewriters against the columns that held up the Sun Tower. By the time Erwin appeared, dodging like O.J. Simpson at the airport, Stu had destroyed twenty-five typewriters. Erwin survived. Stu didn't.

One night, after a fight in the darkroom, John Kirkwood put his fist through a window, occasioning a major flow of claret. Tom Ardies and Nelles Hamilton attempted to drive him the several blocks to the emergency ward of St. Paul's Hospital. Only one problem. They were so blasted, the two best reporters in town, they couldn't remember where it was.

Assistant publisher Himie Koshevoy walked through the women's department, asking how things were "in the Ovary Tower."

Simma Holt, enraged, charged up to Jack Scott at the city desk because of changes in her copy. "What's wrong?" he protested. "I changed only three words." The words were: "By Simma Holt." He fled in panic to the men's loo and locked himself in a cubicle. Simma followed, stood on the throne in the adjoining booth, and beat him over the head.

Tom Ardies, the best reporter on the paper, walked into Erwin's office one day and demanded "a raise or else."

Erwin said, "I think I'll take the or else."

Ardies went back to his desk and started typing.

Fashion editor Marie Moreau was sent to Cuba to interview new dictator Fidel Castro. She got the interview, beating out the astounded world press. On return, a girlfriend asked her if she had slept with Castro. She replied, "How did you think I got the interview?"

Football writer Annis Stukus was sent to Quemoy and Matsu off Formosa (Taiwan), as a third world war was threatening, stopping off first to pose in a tin helmet in a foxhole dug in the English Bay sand by *Sun* photogs.

After the season-end B.C. Lions drunk, Stuke staggered into the sports office with the hot news that the very popular line coach from Texas had been told he was sacked but should go home quietly to Abilene and his retirement would be announced down the track.

When we reported this big-time hypocrisy in our first edition, denials from the Lions filled every radio and TV newscast in town. A hungover Stuke began to question his memory. I, being the nervous kid on the sports desk, had to make a quick decision whether to kill the scoop before the second edition.

Managing editor Hal Straight, all of two hundred and sixty pounds in his $3,000 camel hair topcoat, eventually arrived in the office with casual advice as I babbled the crisis to him: "Kid, don't worry. If you're right, you're right. If you're wrong, you're fired."

It was a dull time.

This is what I came back to.

7
Vancouver and Marriage

When I returned to the *Vancouver Sun*, the managing editor, still Erwin Swangard, put me to work as a sportswriter. Back to the old desk but not for long. One day Swangard told me I was going to be assistant picture editor, which meant I had to sit and write the captions for all of the pictures in the paper.

It seemed like a silly nothing job to me, but I realized later, as I had to fill in for the picture editor on his days off and his holiday, that I would be in on the daily conferences with the top editors and making decisions on how to lay out the front page. He then had me go sit on the "desk" with all of the rheumy old drunks who edited the copy.

Erwin also sent me up to the composing room to instruct the printers how to make up the pages. I finally realized after some time being bounced around like this that he wanted me to learn all of the sections of the paper and all its jobs. While all of my old sportswriter buddies never got out of the sports room.

Swangard had me work in the business department and also spend time writing dull editorials that people never read in any paper. But I learned as an editorial writer that the two most useless words in the English language are *must* and *should*. Every editorial in every newspaper ends up with the words "the government *must* do this or *should* do that." This is like your mother saying you *must* wash behind your ears or you *should not* go out with that boy who arrives on a motorcycle.

While working in the business department I got to know one of the brightest reporters there — a young, very bright woman named Barbara McDougall, who became a good friend throughout her career, including when she became Canada's external affairs minister under Brian Mulroney.

Barbara, her husband, my wife, Sallye (also a reporter at the *Sun*), and I used to go out to Saturday night parties with another couple who were reporters at the same paper. Barbara's husband was an architect — a very nice guy who laughed at anything you said. The only problem was that after three drinks he was on the floor with his eyes rolling over like a Las Vegas slot machine.

Wisely, Barbara ditched him and moved to Edmonton to work for a TV station for Mel Hurtig. She was never legally divorced, and her husband died of a heart attack at an early age because of the gargle. Later, Barbara's political career in Ottawa was greatly enhanced because she was a widow, not a divorced woman. Unlike so many female Cabinet ministers who were seen as failed marriage partners. The fact that she was described in the media as a widow helped her immensely. She is now happily married to former Noranda chairman Adam Zimmerman.

As a senior editor on the editorial page, I shared an office with Pat Carney, an ambitious young business columnist I originally met at *The Ubyssey*. Much later she told me that when she took the bus to the university she was so in awe of me that if I was on the bus she would get off at the next stop. Pat later went on to become a senator and in 1998 married Paul White, the guy who had organized my being chained to the Birks clock.

The third person in our office was a scruffy young man named Bob Hunter, who went on to become one of the founders of Greenpeace and eventually a world leader in the environmental movement. France blew up his protest fishing boat, *The Rainbow Warrior*, in the Pacific Ocean, and Washington, mainly because of the protests he mounted with now millions of Greenpeace members around the globe, agreed to stop all nuclear tests above ground. When he died in the spring of 2005, the parliaments of both Scotland and Japan paid tribute to him.

The managing editor next moved me to run the sports desk. Every day a girl from the Women's Department on the upper floor was sent down to cross the newsroom floor to deliver to the picture editor the photos to run in the women's pages. These little girls, just hired from university, had to walk through the entire newsroom filled with lewd old drunks who harassed them mercilessly, causing them to return to their retreat upstairs almost in tears.

One day I saw one of these girls, very well-dressed, deliver the photos. She was stern in countenance — obviously self-assured and oblivious to the abuse. I asked someone who she was. He said, "Oh, that's that pushy Sallye Delbridge. She shows dogs."

Soon after that an item came in about a dog show. I phoned upstairs to the women's department and asked, "Is there someone up there who knows about dog shows?" They sent Sallye Delbridge down to me. I asked her, "What is it with all these fancy names?" because her dog was named Country Club's Ripple Rock. "What is it with all this hooey?" I was just trying to fake it.

Much later she confessed she had gone home to her dog and said, "I have just met the man I am going to marry." I used to tell this story after we got married at dinner parties, and she'd say, "Yes, but the second time I talked to you I said, 'That is the rudest man I have ever met and never want to see him again.'"

At the time Sallye was engaged to a Rhodes Scholar at Oxford named John Helliwell. He came home from Oxford after two years, and Sallye went to the airport in Vancouver to meet him. Since I assumed she would take him out to dinner and they would have a discussion, I thought it would be some hours before her return.

As it turned out, in those days, before they had walkways into airplanes, people came down the steps to the tarmac. As Helliwell got off the last step, she told him the news and was back at my place in forty-five minutes. He is now a famous economist.

Sallye Delbridge was a single child. She lived at home with her parents for her whole life until she was twenty-six. I was thirty.

I feel sorry for single children because they never learn to share. They never learn to compromise as I did being one of four children — my mother being one of eleven farm children.

When I heard that China, worried about its increasing population, had ordered each family to have only one child, I shuddered — knowing the country was going to raise an entire generation of children that would never know how to compromise, how to share, which has happened. It is the stupidest decision the Chinese government has ever made. The very fact that parents call their children "Little Emperors" indicates that these kids feel it is their way or the highway.

Upon my return from Europe, I was twenty-seven. By twenty-nine, my two sisters and brother were all married with seven children between them. One day I accidentally overheard my mother and stepfather wondering whether I was a homosexual. I decided I had to clarify the situation. I married Sallye Delbridge and was married for seventeen years with three nice children. I was then a bachelor for seventeen years. Until I met my gem. Details to follow. And so much for homosexuality.

In 1962, Sallye was sent to Toronto to work for the *Telegram* for a year. I was dispatched to Western Australia to cover the Commonwealth Games. Prior to my departure, I sent a letter to Sallye's father, Clayton Boston (Slim) Delbridge, asking for her hand in marriage, Sallye and I having discussed this before she went east. After that I travelled to Hiroshima, the site of the first dropping of an atomic bomb, then to Hong Kong, Bangkok, Thailand, Singapore, and finally to Perth in Western Australia to cover the Games as the sports reporter of the *Vancouver Sun*.

Perth is on the shore of the Indian Ocean where I almost drowned in the heavy surf and was saved only by a line shot from the lifeguard station. While covering the Commonwealth Games and planning on going to New Zealand on the way home, I received a letter from Sallye's father saying he would be glad to accept me as the husband of his daughter, but there would have to be a delay since she, working for the *Telegram*, had a stomach hemorrhage and was in the hospital in Toronto. So the marriage plans obviously would have to be delayed until she got better. I flew immediately to Toronto where her mother had been tending her and then brought her back to Vancouver.

As a weird coincidence, when we compared dates, we discovered that Sallye was rushed to the hospital bleeding heavily in Toronto the very same day and eerily the same hour I had almost drowned in Australia. We were married in the spring of 1963.

On the day of the wedding, I was driven to the church in Vancouver by my roommate, Bob Christopher. Several blocks from the church he suddenly realized he was short of gas and pulled into a gas station. The meticulous gas jockey asked whether he would like to have his oil checked. "Sure," Bob said. The guy washed the windshield and checked the tires. All of this useless rigamarole made us late for my own wedding.

Slim Delbridge, standing on the steps of the church with his daughter, with me being fifteen minutes late, said to her, "I warned you he would never show up."

Vancouver and Marriage

Sallye, because she was recovering from her illness, refused to have an ordinary wedding with all of her friends there and stipulated that only the family could attend, with a big party reception at the Delbridge home.

When Sallye discovered she was pregnant, I went to the personnel office of the *Vancouver Sun* to fill out the necessary paperwork needed for medical coverage with a child to come. The personnel director asked when the baby was due. I said, "Well, I understand the usual thinking is nine months from now, but who knows?"

"Well, you know, Allan," she said, "if it arrives in less than nine months from the wedding date, we can't give you coverage."

I looked at her in astonishment. She knew Sallye well, of course, and I said, "I understand your theory that you don't want to hire some young secretary who comes in six months pregnant just to get the coverage."

Giving the toast to the bride, Sallye, at her parents' home.

63

"No," she said, "these are the rules."

I went back down to the newsroom and told my buddies to their great glee that the *Sun* was going to wait to see whether I had an illegitimate child. As the birth of my first son approached, the entire newsroom shouted out the dates as the nine-month deadline approached.

As it happened, Brady Delbridge Fotheringham was born on January 10, 1964, nine months and four days after the wedding. I used to tease Brady by saying he was conceived on an elevator going up to our wedding night room at the Bayshore Inn in Vancouver before taking off the next morning for the honeymoon in Honolulu.

Brady was named after Mathew Brady, a New York photographer who was sent to cover the U.S. Civil War and began to ship longer and longer descriptions of his photos back to New York from the battlefield. They were so good that he was labelled a father of photojournalism. (I think Homer beat him to it.) Decades later Brady took his own photo of himself while in the desert in China, which was used for the front cover of his first book.

Kip Scott Fotheringham arrived two years later on Valentine's Day (Scott being my original paternal surname). Because of my Olympic track dreams, I was a great admirer — I saw him run in London — of Kenya's Kip Keino, who at the time was the world record holder of the mile. So I named my second son after him.

Kip claims that when at school his friends asked him where he got such a crazy name. He explained about Kip Keino and then told them he was glad that the mile record holder at the time wasn't named Mumbo Jumbo from Zanzibar.

Francesca Carmen Fotheringham arrived January 6, three years later, Carmen being Sallye's mother's first name.

Our theory with the names was that Fotheringham being such an awkward, unpronounceable surname, we would give the boys short, quick names. Sallye announced that since our third child would be a girl, she would be named Francesca, shortened to Cesca in everyday use, on the assumption she would marry someone named Smith or Brown. As it turned out, she married Bill Juhasz of Hungarian descent. Which means whenever she goes anywhere, including a bank, she has to spell out both her names. She has never forgiven me.

When Cesca was born, Slim Delbridge asked a friend, "Why would they name the kid after an airplane?" He thought it was Cessna.

After Slim Delbridge was made president of the B.C. Lions, Barry Mather, the front-page columnist of the *News-Herald*, Vancouver's morning paper, wrote a column containing a prediction:

> Slim Delbridge came out of university and got into the Vancouver stock market. He knew nothing about the stock market and ended up a millionaire.
>
> He then became publisher of the *News-Herald*. He knew nothing about newspapers with the result that he ended up with a reporter called Pierre Berton, the best columnist in Canada in Jack Scott and an entire newsroom that was the envy of all of the other Vancouver papers for its staff and the fun they had.
>
> He now has been named president of the B.C. Lions. Slim Delbridge doesn't know a single thing about football. And therefore, I predict he will be the first president to take that club to the Grey Cup and win it.

And he did, beating the Hamilton Tiger-Cats at Exhibition Stadium in Toronto in 1964.

I once was at the Lions' headquarters and asked where Mr. Delbridge's office was. The staff said he had no office there and, in fact, they had never met the man. So I asked Slim about this. He said he had an office in a skyscraper he had built with the backing of John Eaton's money. Slim explained that he didn't even know where the Lions' office was and didn't care.

All he did, he said, was when there was a problem he'd tell the general manager, Herb Capozzi, and the coach, Dave Skrien, to come up to his skyscraper office. That was the way he ran the club — never budging from behind his desk, his six-foot-five frame hunched over it.

Sallye and I sat in the Royal Box at Empire Stadium with her parents for every football game. In the third year she turned to me and confessed she could never figure out which team had the ball. So much for being the president's daughter. Slim probably didn't know, either. Kay Ackles, Bobby's widow, tells me the Lions now have a course for wives to teach them football.

Slim, born in the tough east end of Vancouver, rode his bike six miles every day to the UBC campus. Because he had no money, he paid his way through university by pitching for a semi-pro baseball team and therefore was barred from playing baseball for his university.

Years later, when Sallye and I decided to divorce, he said, "Allan, you are welcome in my home any time you wish." There was a gentleman. Perhaps there was the father I never had. But I digress.

The Southam newspaper chain, which owned the major papers in Canada outside Toronto, announced a yearly scholarship at Massey College, University of Toronto, for four journalists each year. In the second year four of us at the *Vancouver Sun* applied, and to my astonishment, and the resentment of the others, I won. I think I got the scholarship mainly because I emphasized that I was someone from British Columbia who wanted to understand Quebec and its separatist inclinations.

So Sallye and our one-year-old son, Brady, moved to Toronto. While at UBC, Sallye had spent a year as an exchange student at the University of Western Ontario and had become friends with a girl who was now married to Donald MacDonald, then a rising star in the Liberal government in Ottawa.

Because they couldn't afford to keep two homes going in Ottawa and Toronto, they rented us their duplex at Summerhill Gardens in the latter. Don came around once a month as my landlord, and I wrote him a cheque. He has been a friend ever since.

After his first wife, Ruth, died, Don married Adrian Lang. She had been close friends and a next-door neighbour of Ruth and Don in Ottawa and was divorced from Otto Lang, another bright young Cabinet minister from Winnipeg. Adrian and her bright television star daughter, Amanda, are friends of mine to this day, too.

During my Southam scholarship year, I heard about this crazy professor, Marshall McLuhan, who gave a weekly evening lecture that attracted all the high-priced advertising types in Toronto who were intrigued by his theories. I went along every week and was fascinated, even though I didn't understand half of what he was saying.

Vancouver and Marriage

One day I went to the head of my political science department, who had gone to the University of Manitoba with McLuhan and knew him well. "Don't worry, Allan," he said. "Sometimes he goes off into the ozone layer, and I don't know what he's talking about in his lectures for two months. Then he zooms back in and I understand him."

The Southam fellowship involved a close association with the new Massey College, which was designed like an Oxford college. Its first master was Robertson Davies, who would make us dress up on Saturday night in black tie for dinner and then sit around and tell us ghost stories.

Davies was upset because one of the four Southam scholars that year was a woman from the *Calgary Herald*. He said famously, "If you start letting women into Massey, soon there will be ladies with string bags full of cabbages in our presence."

When Sallye and I arrived in Toronto, her father told us to see his close friend, John Bassett, owner of the Toronto Maple Leafs, he having been Sallye's boss at the *Telegram*. I made connections through Bassett's secretary, and the Leafs' owner sent us Saturday night tickets for gold seats — the highest-price ones right behind the Toronto bench.

A month or so later I phoned Bassett's secretary and received two tickets, not in the gold seats but high above. A month or so after that I phoned again, we went to Maple Leaf Gardens, and were handed two tickets. One was high up on the east side of the Gardens; the other was high up on the west side. We got the message.

When the scholarship was finished, Sallye, with Brady, flew back to Vancouver. I decided to educate myself about the United States, got a car, and headed south. All the way to New Orleans. I then turned right and went past the Lyndon Johnson ranch to Houston where I saw the world's first domed stadium.

Continuing west all the way to San Diego, I finally arrived in Vancouver.

I had gone through Selma, Alabama, which was the centre of the civil-rights turmoil and where three white college students who had come down to protest the treatment of blacks were killed. I was warned by someone in town that outsiders like me were either journalists or Washington spies. Somebody dumped sugar in my gas tank, and I had to go to a garage to get the whole engine cleaned out before hightailing it out of town.

Boy from Nowhere

When I returned to the *Vancouver Sun*, they put me back on the editorial page and I had to write those stupid editorials again.

8
Twenty-Six Libel Writs

One day managing editor Bill Galt came to me and said, "You shouldn't be writing editorials, which of course are never signed. You need your own voice." That's when I got my own column, which was in 1968, and I've been writing one ever since.

I was running the op-ed page, soliciting essays, and often contributing a piece of my own. The prime *Vancouver Sun* columnist was Jack Wasserman, who had a terrific following until he quit after a long strike at the paper and moved on to television. Stuart Keate, the publisher, wanted to give the column to sportswriter Denny Boyd, who was a favourite of Keate's because they both came from the *Victoria Times*.

Because Swangard knew something that neither Keate nor I knew, he disagreed and said, "If you give Boyd that job, he'll be an alcoholic in six months," because the job mainly entailed going out and covering the nightclubs in the evening for items.

Swangard had seen Denny on football trips across the country and apparently had watched him get into trouble with all the free booze. As it turned out, Swangard was right. Within months Denny came in from his all-night roaming and his columns began to appear full of chicken scratches and misspellings. By this time, I had been doing his column on his day off once a week and whenever he went on holidays.

One early morning Denny came in, went into his office, and typed out his column. When he handed it in, it was completely incomprehensible, the whole thing looking as if a cat had walked over the typewriter keys. Boyd was dismissed, and I was called in the next day and asked to do the column permanently by managing editor Galt. That was in 1968, the year Pierre Trudeau became prime minister.

I had seen in the *Seattle Post-Intelligencer* a column written by a guy who sat in on city council meetings and remarked about some woman's lipstick, the cheap suit one of the men wore, and it was hilarious. So I decided to do the same thing in the *Vancouver Sun*.

Boy from Nowhere

Every Monday I went to City Hall and sat there from 10:00 a.m. to 6:00 p.m., taking notes about what everyone wore, how they looked, everything except the issues they were discussing. This caused a sensation both in the newsroom and among readers because no one had ever approached politics that way. I never went to the nightclubs or restaurants that my predecessor frequented.

When Muhammad Ali came to town, I interviewed him. I attended Vancouver Canucks hockey games and described how Bobby Orr skated — the finest player in the world at the time. This unusual way of doing a column meant I typed in my office in the basement close to midnight, which really helped my marriage.

I walked the length of Granville Street and described everything I saw — every shop, every store. And the readers loved it. So did my editors.

I wrote five columns a week for nine years and then cut back to three columns a week, attempting to save my marriage. The attempt obviously didn't work. There was also another reason.

Jack Wasserman was the most popular columnist because he wrote in the Walter Winchell style — lots of dot-dot-dots, lots of different items,

One of the many billboards in and around Vancouver while I was at the Vancouver Sun.

lots of names in bold face. Jack wrote five columns a week for years before briefly going to TV. His father had been a scrap dealer. He collected the garbage with a horse and buggy. Wasserman was a heavy smoker and drinker and was basically insecure.

One night there was a black tie tribute to Gordon Gibson, Sr., a famous B.C. forestry figure, at the Hyatt Hotel in Vancouver. Everybody who was anybody in town was there (except me) from the mayor on down. Over too many drinks beforehand, Jack Webster, Wasserman's close friend, teased the *Sun* columnist relentlessly because Wasserman had to give the first speech and Jack was going to be the mop-up star attraction.

Wasserman stood at the podium and started to tell a joke. He got to the punch line and suddenly pitched forward over the microphone. The whole room laughed, thinking this was part of the act. Wasserman was dead before he hit the floor. He was fifty years old. I decided I didn't want to go that route, so I cut back my column to three a week.

I wasn't at the Wasserman affair because of a family dispute and was at the typewriter as usual close to midnight when the phone rang. It was Jack Webster. "I was there when he died," he said.

"Who died?" I asked.

"Wasserman."

Years later, in front of Webster and friends, I dined out with that story. It was a typical example of his ego. Jack thought the story was that *he* was there. Wasserman came in second.

Wasserman, being a Jew, was immediately cremated. His ashes were on hand for a memorial service. At the service Herb Capozzi, the B.C. Lions' general manager, surreptitiously stole a handful of ashes and put it in his suit pocket. To Herb's horror, the next week his wife sent the suit to the cleaners. Later, he boasted to everyone: "Wasserman was born circumcised and ended up sanitized."

I'm quite proud of attracting more libel suits than any journalist in Canadian history. Mainly because I told the truth and made Peter Butler, the *Vancouver Sun*'s legal adviser, rich. Stu Keate, the *Sun*'s publisher, boasted that in one day he received three libel writs from three different people on my columns. He thought that was probably a world record.

Every time he got a writ he'd call me into his office and ask, "Can you back this up?"

"Yep," I'd say.

"Okay. Call in Mr. Butler."

I had twenty-six libel writs and won twenty-four of them. Most of the offended politicians, of course, never showed up in court after getting all of their publicity. The only two suits I lost were with my column in *Maclean's*, where I was defended by my close friend, Julian Porter, husband of Anna Porter, who published eight books of mine.

Peter Butler and I became good friends. My kids played with his kids, and we went down to his holiday home in Point Roberts, just across the B.C. border in Washington State. He even dropped in at my house for breakfast sometimes on the way to his law office downtown. So it was with some surprise that I walked into a Vancouver courtroom to see Butler across the floor representing the two John Turner executive assistants who were suing me.

At one stage Butler said, "Mr. Fotheringham, I suggest you've never apologized for a single column you've ever written."

John Turner and I on the Liberal Party campaign plane.

"Mr. Butler," I replied, "you know that's not true because you gave my paper the advice on every single one of them."

I thought the judge was suffering from whiplash. He jerked his head at news he obviously didn't know.

Julian Porter, son of former Ontario Chief Justice Dana Porter, had come out from Toronto and was wearing his father's faded judicial robes, eager for Toronto's most famous libel lawyer to take on Vancouver's most famous libel lawyer. It was like a bullfight.

Julian got up, gave his oration, then sat down with a magnificent flourish, throwing the tails of his father's robe behind him. As you can imagine, every single reporter on the three Vancouver newspapers were in the courtroom, wanting to see Fotheringham cut down to size. They laughed at this flourish from the big Toronto hotshot.

Butler, knowing what he was doing, always looked as if he had just gotten out of bed. His hair was never combed, he wore a shabby gown, and after Julian had done his robe flourish for the sixth time, I knew we were dead. The two executive assistants got $10,000 on the judgment. To this day I don't know why the judge didn't advise the plaintiffs to get another lawyer to represent them due to conflict of interest.

I should point out that the suit was over a column in which I said the two young Turner aides, one of whom happened to be a friend of mine and had succeeded me as editor of *The Ubyssey*, had risen very quickly as young lawyers in "the tennis club, wife-swapping areas" of the richer ridings in Vancouver.

What I didn't know was that the two lawyers and their wives were close friends and shared a summer cottage on one of the Gulf Islands, thereby giving their friends who knew of the cottage the clear inference that I was suggesting they were actual wife swappers. I was using *wife swapping* as a generic term.

After the verdict came down, I was at the annual Christmas party at the Vancouver Tennis and Badminton Club and another lawyer, Rae Ross, a friend, came up and said, "Foth, you should have talked to me. I could name three couples in this club alone."

My second loss was to explorer Sir Ranulph Twisleton-Wykeham-Fiennes, who was one of those rich English twits who attempted to walk to the North Pole and do other silly things. A great sponsor of his was Prince

Boy from Nowhere

Charles. He came to British Columbia advertising he was going to retrace the route of the mighty Fraser River from its source to its outfall into the Pacific. Fiennes brought a small troop of eight British soldiers with him.

Vancouver Sun reporter Moira Farrow followed him on the latter stages of this so-called dangerous expedition. She came back and told me all the intimate stuff she couldn't report on this tremendous expedition that got so much local publicity. He treated these "lower-class" soldiers — as opposed to his Oxford-educated class — like dirt, giving them lousy rations while he dined on champagne.

There was almost open rebellion from the poorly paid soldiers, and Moira thought Fiennes was lucky to get to Vancouver and the fancy TV publicity as the Fraser emptied its muddy waters into the blue Pacific.

I wrote a column in *Maclean's*, describing him and his phony expedition, and said he'd never done anything that had any historical or geographical significance. Fiennes sued *Maclean's* and me. Several years went by, and I had forgotten all about it, thinking his charges were ridiculous because, among other things, *Maclean's* had only maybe twenty copies of each issue in the whole British Isles, mainly shipped to school libraries.

Therefore, I was somewhat astonished one day two years later when travelling from Italy I arrived in London to see splashed on the second page of London's *Daily Mail*, along with my picture, a big report about the previous day's opening of the trial in a London courtroom. For some strange reason Julian Porter, the *Maclean's* lawyer, had decided not to contest the case, apparently thinking it would die naturally. And I guess save *Maclean's* a lot of money by not shipping Julian to London.

Naturally, I went to the court the second day of the trial and got there as the prosecutor thundered, "And where is Kevin Doyle, editor of *Maclean's*? Why is he not here? Where is Mr. Fotheringham? Why is he not here?"

I scrunched down in the tiny public gallery, which had only six seats, when I spotted a burly chap in the jury, all of whom had been supplied with the back page of *Maclean's*. He glanced up at me, looked down at his copy several times, then started nudging the other jurors, who all looked up at the public galley. I put the *Times* of London over my face. Too late. The case was lost, and *Maclean's* paid the explorer $200,000 in damages and $150,000 in legal costs.

In any event, as the years went by, my column became very popular. And my influence grew both inside and outside the paper. I was credited with overthrowing through my vicious columns the long-time TEAM government that ruled City Hall for too long. And I wrote six consecutive columns on Highways Minister Reverend Phil Gaglardi, forcing his resignation.

At the *Vancouver Sun* my position was strengthening but my desire to write a column so often was fading. The morale at the paper was at an all-time low. In the process I made it known how I felt. There were a number of energetic, educated people working there who didn't have the sense that they were getting anywhere due to the old-school, lewd drunks still dominating the newsroom.

Therefore I took it upon myself to send a long six-page memo to publisher Stu Keate, outlining my concerns and offering suggestions. As a result, Stu made up a new position and called it "senior editor." He made me the senior editor along with Dave Ablett, another bright up-and-comer. No one knew exactly what the term meant.

But the change of title rankled Bruce Larsen, the managing editor, especially when Ablett and I were placed above him on the masthead. This exacerbated his negative feelings toward me. I, of course, thought I could make the paper better and improve its morale. Instead a power struggle ensued.

Around this time, 1975, I received a letter from Peter C. Newman, the new editor of *Maclean's*. He wanted me to move to Ottawa and be the magazine's bureau chief. My wife wouldn't hear of it. But Newman asked me to fly to Toronto to discuss the concept further.

I did so and told Newman I couldn't move from Vancouver but would write a column from there for him. Newman called in his senior editors, Walter Stewart and John Macfarlane, and some other staff and asked them their thoughts on whether I could write such a column from Vancouver.

"Foth, we love you," said Stewart, "but no frigging way. You can't cover Canada from Lotusland."

Newman went around the table, and each editor reiterated Stewart's opinion. Then he sat back, smoked his pipe, and said, "You're all wrong. It may not be a national column, but it will be a Fotheringham column. Foth, file your first column next week."

I flew back to Vancouver, wrote my first *Maclean's* column, and submitted it. On Tuesday I rushed out to the newsstand and, being a man of small ego, assumed it would be on page three or four at least. It wasn't on page ten, fifteen, or twenty-five. I still remember thinking, *Shit, it wasn't good enough.* I riffled through the rest of the magazine, only to find my column on the back page — the most brilliant positioning in Canadian journalism. (*Time* and then *Newsweek* followed suit two years later. Today most magazines have columns on their back pages.) And Canadians began to read *Maclean's* back to front.

Then the offers started to come in. I began doing guest appearances on various news shows on television, one being *the fifth estate* on CBC. On one of these Toronto appearances I was identified as the "editor" of the *Vancouver Sun,* as opposed to the senior editor. Bruce Larsen went ballistic and screaming to Stu Keate. Between editions a burly pressman chiselled my name off the masthead.

The next evening I went back to Vancouver. When I got off the plane from Toronto and arrived home, I told my wife I'd been fired as the *Sun's*

The Vancouver Show *on CKVU-TV. Myself, Pia Shandel, Emmanuelle Gattuso (the producer), Sandy Ross, and Laurier LaPierre in the front.*

senior editor. Sallye, washing the dishes at the time, didn't even turn around. She said, "Good. Now you can get back to what you're good at."

I returned to writing a column for the *Vancouver Sun* three times a week and doing special assignments. I carried on with *Maclean's* for the next twenty-seven years. And I took a position as an occasional commentator at Vancouver television station CKVU where I discussed politics after the evening news.

Then my life took another direction.

Stuart Keate retired from the *Vancouver Sun* in 1978 at the age of sixty-five, and the paper hired Clark Davey, managing editor of the *Globe and Mail*, to be its new publisher. As he was leaving the *Globe*, Davey told his staff that the first thing he was going to do was to show Fotheringham that every paper could have only one star and he was going to be it. Within six months I was gone.

9
Hitting $492,000

Roy Peterson illustrated my back page in *Maclean's* and won three straight National Newspaper Awards. We had this funny little stubborn view that we were the best columnist and cartoonist in the country and would show Toronto we didn't have to go to Hogtown. Roy and I held that opinion for years until I gave in and moved east in 1980.

My dilemma of being torn between East and West as a journalist was finally solved strangely and understandably enough by two foreigners, one a pugnacious Australian and the other a pushy Englishman. Neither of them was soiled by a university education.

They being strangers to the land, of course, they knew nothing about the hatred Vancouver had for Toronto. The pair simply regarded me as a valuable product to be seduced to where the big markets were — eastern Canada, Toronto, Ottawa. They hired me away and in doing so eventually ended my marriage.

As I mentioned earlier, after I started writing a column for the *Vancouver Sun* in 1968, offers came from the hotshots in central Canada. The CBC wanted me to come to Toronto to be on a TV show. At one point in the mid-1970s, according to *Saturday Night* magazine, the *Toronto Star* "was so convinced it had landed him that it rented billboard space to announce it. Foth balked at the last moment."

Global Television's Jeremy Brown, with whom I had gone to university, came to Vancouver to have lunch with me at the Bayshore Inn and offered me a job at $75,000 per annum. I was then making about $35,000 at the *Vancouver Sun*. I thought he was insane to offer me that much money.

To prove he could, he pulled out a pay sheet and showed he was being paid $90,000 a year and that his boss, Bill Cunningham, was earning $125,000 a year. I thought they were crazy and turned down the offer. Shortly thereafter, Global went bankrupt and was bought by Izzy Asper and Gerry Schwartz. Bruce Garvey and Ray Heard said they had to get Foth for Global TV. Again I was approached. In the end Global did have me as a regular commentator, though I was never on staff.

Eventually, Ted Bolwell, an Australian who I had met years before when he was the *Globe and Mail* man in Vancouver, started something called FP News Service in Ottawa.

To induce me to move to Ottawa, he said FP would buy a condo for me in the classiest section of the city and I could come for two weeks a month and then retreat to Vancouver, since my wife refused to move east. That would allow Sallye and our children to come to the nation's capital whenever they wanted to.

I thought Sallye and I had an agreement that we would try it for a year, then decide on either Ottawa or Vancouver as our permanent home. But after eight months, understandably weary from putting up with a part-time husband, she quietly asked, "This marriage isn't working, is it?"

We hired lawyer Peter Butler to represent both of us (a bad decision) and had a quiet (but difficult) divorce to keep it away from the gossip columns. After seventeen years. With three nice kids. In my naïveté I thought Butler would deal with the situation in the best interests of both parties. I was later told he was remorseful after the divorce was complete, since he knew he had deliberately given me a life sentence. He did it out of resentment that I was getting all of the publicity with my writing and he felt he should be the hotshot in town. To this day I send my ex-wife a monthly cheque. More than thirty years later. Ultimately, Butler wound up in a wheelchair with a rare disease in his final years.

I rented an apartment in Vancouver and continued with the arrangement of travelling between Ontario and British Columbia so I could spend time with my children but still work at FP News Service. Bolwell's FP was owned by the Thomson family and had the finest reporting staff in Ottawa: Carol Goar, Walter Stewart, and Mary Janigan, to name three.

A rumour went around that the bureau was going to be killed. So I went down to Toronto to talk to the head Thomson guy, St. Clair McCabe, and explained that we had the best bureau in Ottawa and we were all worried about the rumours and had offers from everybody else.

He listened to me for an hour, then said, "I don't know what you're worried about, Mr. Fotheringale."

I went back to Ottawa and told the troops, "It's over." And I moved to Southam News.

I had been approached by the major newspapers in Canada, so I contacted the chairman of Southam, the largest newspaper chain in the land. I said I would come to them with one provision: I had to have an outlet in Toronto. I knew very well that Charles Lynch, who had been the star Southam columnist for decades, was known in every Canadian Legion hall in Canada, but no one in Toronto had ever heard of him. The chairman agreed and said he would get me into the *Toronto Star*.

Gossip being everything in the newspaper business, Richard Gwyn, who had been a good friend of mine, heard about the *Star* possibility and immediately got the idea killed. Which was rather strange since he wrote a rather serious, well-thought-out political column and my gig was dancing around and humorous — Art Buchwald crossed with William Safire and Pete Hamill.

The *Toronto Sun* heard about the *Star* turndown and phoned me — and I got my Toronto outlet. (Like Charlie Lynch, I guess Richard Gwyn thought he was the star of the *Toronto Star* and didn't want any competition.) So now I had a column in the Southam papers, the *Toronto Sun*, and *The Financial Post*, which the *Sun* organization owned.

The day I got the contract Bill Fox, who was in Pierre Trudeau's office, came into the National Press Gallery bar in the National News Building and grabbed me by the arm. "Do you know what you've just done?" he asked. "With your column in *Maclean's* and now your column in all of the major Southam papers, including Montreal, Ottawa, Regina, Saskatoon, Edmonton, Calgary, and Vancouver, you'll have the biggest readership any Canadian columnist has ever had."

I had never thought of it that way, but he was right. That was the start of the 1980s for me.

Nick Hills was my boss at Southam. He was an indescribable, excitable boy from England who showed up in Vancouver as the Southam News correspondent. He had previously been managing editor of the *Winnipeg Free Press*.

Nick lasted there for several years under the Winnipeg weather until finally one day he walked into a Thomas Cook travel agency in Winnipeg in the middle of a bitter winter and said, "Show me on your globe the farthest spot in the world from Winnipeg." It turned out to be New Zealand.

He flew to New Zealand, immediately got a position as an editor on the Auckland paper, and spied a beautiful young redhead reporter named Lana, then sent her out on interesting assignments. Not surprisingly, he took up with her, married her, and flew her back to Winnipeg in the dead of winter, she wearing only a raincoat.

After a stint as London correspondent, Nick came back to Ottawa as general manager of Southam News, hence, my boss. He and Lana were having marriage problems, and they moved into my Southam digs with me. Recently separated myself, I tried to warn them about the dangers of destruction.

Knowing Nick's position and knowing that half of Ottawa was franco-phone, Lana wisely said she should learn French and that Southam should pay to send her to a French immersion course in Switzerland, which the company did. At the immersion school she met Richard Underhill, who had been president of the student council of UBC when I was the editor of *The Ubyssey*.

Nick left for Val-d'Isère in France to pick Lana up, and she informed him they were not only going to get divorced but she was marrying Richard Underhill. (You can't make that up: leaving Hills for an Underhill.) Nick and Lana went to Paris to have dinner with the Southam correspondent, a close friend of theirs. They sat there in a beautiful Parisian restaurant the whole evening, with Nick, his face in his plate, not saying a word, their host not knowing the marriage was over after twenty-five years.

Lana has been a close friend of mine ever since and, in fact, is the reason I've been going to Bowen Island in British Columbia in the summer for thirty years, she in her new marriage inviting me there, me being just divorced in 1981.

* * *

Boy from Nowhere

In 1983 son Kip's high school rugby team headed off to play a series of matches in England and Scotland against British youngsters. I went with them, thinking that would make a good father/son column-writing gig. Partway through the tour, in Scotland at half-time of one game, I thought I should finally put in a call to the Southam office.

I phoned Nick Hills in Ottawa. "Just checking in," I said. "Is anything happening?"

In his usual deadpan manner, Nick said, "No, not much. You've just been named the first winner of the National Newspaper Award for Column Writing and we're shipping you to Washington."

With Kip's team I moved down to London and called Shirley Eskapa, a writer I'd met in Portugal. She and her husband threw a lovely dinner for me with an intelligent group of journalist friends. I told them I'd just been invited to go to Washington, but I hadn't accepted yet because I was worried I'd be far away from my children.

They looked at me as if I was a moron, saying I was crazy to fuss about being assigned to the most powerful city in the world. They were right, of course. I can't believe now that I even hesitated over the choice.

But let me explain. In 1966, when Kip was born, Sallye suffered post-partum depression. She was taken to Hawaii by her aunt to recover. While there a young man sent a ransom note to my in-laws demanding money or he'd kill their grandchildren, my three children.

At the same time the *Vancouver Sun*'s Washington correspondent, who apparently hadn't paid his American income tax, had to get out of the United States immediately and therefore the paper needed me to succeed him immediately.

Here I was, thirty-four years old with my wife in Hawaii, receiving a kidnapping threat. I desperately tried to warn my wife's aunt to cut out of the Vancouver papers — which arrived in Honolulu every day on Canadian Pacific Airlines flights — any reference to this situation to protect Sallye. (Eventually, the police were able to apprehend the man, and my family was safe from any further cause for concern.)

So obviously, under those circumstances, I couldn't accept that juicy offer in the 1960s to go to Washington. It took until 1983, seventeen years later, before I was offered the position again. This time I went. Such is life.

Hitting $492,000

I arrived in Washington in 1984, three years after Allan Gotlieb became Canadian ambassador to the United States. He and his eccentric wife, Sondra, were friends from my Ottawa days. Twenty Canadian correspondents were covering Washington then — CBC, Canadian Press, the *Globe and Mail*, the *Toronto Star*, et cetera. And the Gotliebs, by accident, became hosts of the hottest embassy in town.

The most powerful city in the world, of course, is inundated with embassies representing more than a hundred countries. Washington insiders, White House types, power journalists, heavyweight lobbyists work very hard (much harder than Canadians, this scribbler quickly learned).

All those movers and shakers want one place at 5:00 p.m. they can go to until 7:00 p.m. to learn over a quick drink who's going up and who's going down in the pecking order, who's screwing whom, who's about to be fired — one stop where they can get all the dirt. As the wise man once said, the definition of gossip is "organized information."

To get all this precious stuff, Washington insiders pick out one embassy — and it's never the Indonesian embassy or the Bolivian one. As Allan explained once, when he arrived in town, Sir Nicky Henderson was leaving. Henderson was the charming British ambassador with a wonderful kitchen and bar that attracted every one of the capital's hot informers to his place each afternoon at five sharp.

Such a man was hard to follow but, as Allan candidly confessed, there was a vacuum for the gossipers, and the Gotliebs — the *Toronto Star*'s Richard Gwyn helping with the contacts — inherited by accident the hot embassy locale vacated by Sir Nicky.

On any given evening at the Canadian embassy, I might find myself sitting down to dinner with Henry Kissinger across the table, Defense Secretary Caspar Weinberger beside him. David Brinkley might be lingering about, along with Meg Greenfield, the op-ed editor of the *Washington Post*, and Katharine Graham, the *Post*'s owner and publisher. Peter Jennings and Dan Rather wouldn't be far away, either.

The Gotliebs became hosts of the hottest embassy because Allan was so bright and Sondra was so goofy. She used to butt her cigarettes in the salt cellar at the table. The gossip columnists absolutely loved her. The Gotlieb rule was that they would invite each of the twenty Canadian correspondents to one dinner evening a year. But I was there every single night at their dinner parties. Which, of course, is why I was hated by all the Canadian reporters in town.

In 1986 the Gotliebs had the biggest party in their career. Prime Minister Brian Mulroney, Vice President George Bush, Sr., and I were seated inside at the table, while all the other Canadian press, pissed off, of course, had to stand outside in the street. That was the evening Sondra, on the patio in front of everyone, slugged Connie Connor, depositing Connie's earring into the bushes.

The next day I had to fly to Winnipeg to make a speech, and a CBC reporter tracked me down at my hotel and asked, "Mr. Fotheringham, we understand you were at the Gotliebs' last night?"

"Yes," I said.

"Could you tell us about Mrs. Gotlieb slugging her maid?"

"What are you talking about?"

"Well, we've just read a Canadian Press dispatch saying she slugged her maid, Connie Connor."

"That isn't her maid," I said. "That's her social secretary."

I'd missed the biggest scoop of the year.

Later, I learned that Ambassador Gotlieb went to Mulroney's hotel at midnight and offered to resign. It was declined. Sondra Gotlieb, in her subsequent book (*Washington Rollercoaster*), said I was responsible for leaking the information that made her into an idiot.

When I spoke with Connie Connor at a later date, she informed me that the reason she was slugged was because, on such a tense evening, she hadn't informed the ambassador's wife that one of the star guests was going to be late, and it all happened in full view of the twenty Canadian reporters outside the embassy. Connie told me, "You know who was responsible for that, Allan? His name was Mr. Smirnoff."

As can be imagined, there are thousands of reporters from every semi-civilized country in the world in Washington covering the White House. At presidential press conferences a polite young lady always came up to me, sitting well in the back rows, to inquire who I was and what paper I represented. "Southam News of Canada," I'd tell her, watching her write it down.

As can be imagined, never once in a million years does the president recognize someone like me raising his hand for a question. Who knows what I might ask? Is it true you secretly smoke dope?

All of the questions go, naturally, to the trusted ones. "Yes, Sam," the president says to Sam Donaldson. "Yes, Cokie," he says to Cokie Roberts. The questions go to NBC, ABC, the *New York Times*, Associated Press. All the correspondents the president knows would never block the copy book by asking something that would make rude headlines the next day. The foreigners, though, are shut out because they might ask something outside the box. All of us, knowing the rules, had to accept them, which is why lads like Geraldo Rivera end up late at night on Fox News when no one is watching.

When I arrived in Washington for five glorious years in the most powerful city on the globe, I found a house in Georgetown on Dent Place. It was two blocks beneath the mansion of the *Washington Post*'s Katharine Graham. It was also two blocks above Bob Woodward's home on the Georgetown slope.

I had met Woodward, of Woodward and Bernstein fame who brought down Richard Nixon with the Watergate scandal, in Vietnam where we drank in the Hanoi Hilton with someone else who became famous — Pulitzer Prize winner David Halberstam. In Washington, Woodward and I shared a woman. Both of us being bachelors and busy beyond belief, neither one of us knew how to properly throw a dinner party.

We found a very cute young lady who, whenever either of us was having a dinner party for all the hotshots in town, would go out, do all the shopping, come and cook the meal, serve the meal, clean up the kitchen, and go home. A dastardly reporter from the *Boston Globe* wooed and won her, married her, and took her home to Boston. Woodward and I have hated him ever since.

I had just moved to Washington when Gordon Sinclair died at age eighty-three, he being the long-standing and most controversial member of the most popular show on the CBC, *Front Page Challenge*, which ran for thirty-nine years. *Front Page Challenge* featured four top journalists as a panel guessing the identity of a hidden mystery guest — a top politician, a well-known entertainment figure, a famous athlete — and then questioning

Boy from Nowhere

them. I had appeared several times as a guest panellist whenever the show was shot in Vancouver. When Gordon died, I thought, modestly, that the CBC would ask me to replace him.

Several weeks went by, and one day I was in the shower when I picked up the phone and it was Ray McConnell, boss of the show. I didn't even say hello, since I knew why he was calling. "Why did it take you so long to call?" I asked.

Apparently, I wasn't the first choice as Sinclair's replacement. The first choice was Pierre Trudeau, only recently no longer the prime minister. That fell apart, strangely enough, because of millionaire Trudeau's demand for money that the program's budget couldn't accommodate.

The second choice was Jack Webster, the blustering Scottish Vancouver talk show host who couldn't accept because he worked for rival CTV. When the announcement about me was made, Webster, a close friend, blustered across the land that I had been the second choice next to him. As I explained to everyone at the time, I wasn't the second choice. I was the third choice. Webster had been the second choice.

I lasted ten years with *Front Page Challenge*.

Gordon Sinclair, Betty Kennedy, myself, and Pierre Berton guessing B.C. Premier Dave Barrett on Front Page Challenge. *Courtesy of Vancouver's* Province.

Hitting $492,000

Gordon Sinclair had always made headlines, highlighted by the time he questioned mystery guest Elaine Tanner, the swimmer who had just come back as an Olympic medallist. She was the sweetheart of the nation. She was eighteen years old. And Sinclair asked her how she coped with her menstrual periods when she was training so hard. There were motions in the House of Commons the next day to force the CBC to fire him.

One of the historic nights of the show was when Winston Churchill's daughter, Sarah, showed up as a star mystery guest and was completely blotto. In fact, the terrified staff, headed by Lorraine Thomson, found her outside on Yonge Street in the middle of a downpour without a coat on directing traffic. They eventually took her into the green room and poured gallons of coffee down her before the show in an attempt to get her sober. It didn't work.

One time, Pierre Berton had to go to Australia on journalistic assignment. Sinclair warned him this was a stupid idea because he couldn't possibly get back in time to do the show. What he didn't know was that they had arranged for Berton to be the mystery guest on the next program. The panellists never got him.

Gordie Howe, one of the finest hockey players in the NHL, appeared as the mystery guest six times. And fooled them each time.

We taped the show every week in a different city, from St. John's to Victoria, which meant I had to fly up from Washington every week and see another city in Canada. Bruce Phillips, a prominent Ottawa columnist, got Press Club laughs with the line that "Fotheringham is covering Washington from inside a CBC studio in Canada."

As might be expected, a party was thrown after each show by the locals, who were thrilled to see such famous people as Berton and Sinclair. After a few drinks, Pierre, who was born in Dawson City, would get up and recite "The Shooting of Dan McGrew," accompanied by full theatrics, including falling dead with his six-foot-three frame onto the carpet floor while the locals gasped in astonishment.

One day we were leaving for the Halifax airport at seven in the morning after the previous night's *Front Page Challenge*. As we crossed a bridge, the grizzled taxi driver pointed out a large ship in the harbour and said, "That's a cruiser."

The rest of us were half asleep, but Berton said, "No, it's not. It's a 947B destroyer." Then, off the top of his head, he recited all the names and numbers of the ships in the Canadian and British navies. By the time we reached the airport, the grizzled old taxi driver hadn't said another word.

After ten years, I was phoned one day by the CBC and was told, with a lawyer listening, that *Front Page Challenge* was being killed. Pierre Berton, the longest-serving panellist on the show from the day it debuted, learned about the closing from his secretary. Until the day he died, he was never personally contacted by a CBC executive.

The head of CBC programming, Ray McConnell, announced he would mount a farewell lunch for the cast, which included long-time panellist Betty Kennedy and emcee Fred Davis. I wrote a vicious column about the crude, unfeeling way the CBC had treated its biggest stars. Guess what McConnell did? He cancelled the lunch. That's why we call the network the Canadian Broadcorping Castration.

My move to *Front Page Challenge* meant I now had five jobs. In addition to a national newspaper column and the weekly column in *Maclean's*, I had published three of my eight books and was on the lecture circuit across the country. This led Peter C. Newman, who apparently knew such things, to announce that I was the highest-paid working journalist in Canada, with an annual income past $400,000. In fact, one year I nudged a cool half-million. My income tax return confessed to $492,000.

10
Toronto Sun Days

There is an old saying in the trade that you'll never become a millionaire being a newspaperman, but you can live like one. I believe I was the first working journalist in Canada to break the rule.

Because I had five jobs — that national newspaper column, the *Maclean's* column, *Front Page Challenge*, Key Porter turning out eight of my books, and my being on the lecture circuit — it meant I had five employers. And if one of them didn't like my expense account, there were always four others.

The standard dream of every newspaper bloke is to be assigned by his paper to a fancy story far away — to another continent if possible. The assignments came so rare and in between in an average career. It all depended on the boss.

By my Irish luck, I turned the relationship upside down. I never had to wait for an assignment. I decided where I wanted to go. One of the five (or all of them occasionally) would pay the freight.

Visiting the Great Wall of China. Decades later my son, Brady, did the same.

Boy from Nowhere

I got to know every European country: Scandinavia, Poland, Russia, the Baltic states. I did Africa from top to bottom. South America from top to bottom. China, Japan, and Korea. Down through Vietnam, Malaysia, the Philippines, India, Australia, forty-eight of the fifty U.S. states. In all, ninety-one countries. The only place I missed was New Zealand, for reasons explained earlier.

So I became the most hated (i.e., envied) typist among all my comrades in our racket in Canada because I was in control of my own fate.

While in Washington I tried to take each of my children along with me on one of my journeys at least once a year. On one occasion I travelled to Israel. My daughter, Cesca, actually asked if she could go along. We arrived in Jerusalem and checked into the King David Hotel.

The next morning my inquisitive daughter, sixteen at the time, announced, as any bright youngster will do upon arrival in a new and interesting city, that she was going to roam the town to get a feel for it. I said I didn't think that was a good idea.

Several hours later the *Jerusalem Post* was shoved under the hotel room door. On the front page was the story of how the previous day two young Arab girls dressed in robes were in the city market when they suddenly pulled out large knives and stabbed an elderly tourist to death,

Floating in the Dead Sea in Israel while reading my newspaper — priorities!

a German who turned out to be completely innocent. After that, Cesca, who is gorgeous and blond, decided she would stick close to Daddy and that it wasn't wise to wander a religious city alone.

Back then the major issue in Canada was a proposal to build an oil pipeline from the Northwest Territories to the southern part of the country and then ship the fuel to the United States, thus cutting American reliance on Middle East oil. Ottawa appointed Tom Berger, a very serious Vancouver lawyer I had gone to university with, as a one-man commission to go to the North and deliver a report on the pipeline's feasibility. I went along with Berger and took my son, Brady, who was then a teenager. With Berger's staff, one of whom is now a judge in the Ontario Superior Court, we slept on the floor of log cabins in the Northwest Territories.

Berger's assistant was Diana Crosbie, a smart and pretty Toronto public relations person. She once came over and crawled into the window of our abode. When Brady returned home, he told his mother. As innocent as it was, you can well imagine that Sallye wasn't amused.

Berger, as we know, turned down the pipeline because of Native objections and what it would do to destroy caribou herds. Construction of the pipeline was delayed, but it went ahead twenty years later. Berger eventually became a member of the Supreme Court of Canada.

I was in Washington until 1989. The stint came to an end when my boss, Nick Hills, paid me a visit in the U.S. capital one day. We went out to lunch next door to the National Press Building and had our usual martini-filled lies and jokes and hilarious lunch at the end of which he reached into his jacket and pulled out a letter that said: "This will inform you that your employment at Southam News will finish on December 31, 1989."

At first I thought it was a typical Nick Hills joke. But, apparently, he didn't think so. More recently in Paris in May 2006 I ran into Paddy Sherman, the chairman of Southam News in 1989, and learned that he had understood the letter was supposed to be a simple attempt to reduce my exorbitant salary. Sherman had no idea that Hills had actually written the letter as a termination. But I still have the letter in my files.

Boy from Nowhere

So I phoned my agent, Perry Goldsmith, and told him I would take up the long-standing invitation from Doug Creighton at *The Financial Post*. The next week Creighton came down to Washington, took me to dinner at the Four Seasons Hotel in Georgetown, and hired me.

One of the most unusual and surprising people I've ever met is Doug Creighton, who I thought was just an uneducated cop shop reporter at Toronto's *Telegram*. When that paper was folded in 1971 by John Bassett on a Saturday, Creighton, along with partners Peter Worthington and Donald Hunt, somehow gathered enough money from backers, took the *Telegram*'s staff into a cheap old building filled with orange crates, and put out the *Toronto Sun* by Monday morning.

I got to know Doug a bit because he wasn't afraid of anybody and had twice asked me to be the editor of the *Sun*. I kept turning him down until that fateful day in Washington when I was let go by Southam. By this time, Creighton also owned *The Financial Post*, which for twelve years I wrote a column.

One day in the early 1990s, since Creighton was famous for his lunches, he took me to Winston's, the hangout of all of the Toronto Establishment figures. It was January, and he asked me what my travel plans were for the year. I said, "I hadn't really thought about it yet." And he said he had an idea.

The idea was that I would go and find the ten richest resorts in the world. Doug said, "There are two types of people. The rich people who have been to all those resorts and will either agree or disagree with you. The other people are those who have never been out of Canada in their lives and dream of winning the lottery so they can see London, Paris, and Rome."

At first I thought he was kidding, but when we got back to the office, within twenty minutes, I ran into Doug's executive assistant, Lynn Carpenter, and she excitedly said I had to give her dates, locations, et cetera. I thought rumours really ran quickly around that joint and asked her where she'd heard this news. "Oh, from Doug," she said.

Several days later, after the dream assignment had sunk in, I went to Creighton and said, "Look, if I go to all these resorts, they'll be filled with rich American couples, rich British couples, rich German couples. And I'll have nothing to do but sit there talking to the bartender with no partner to play doubles tennis with."

"Oh, sure," he said, "I realize that. Take anyone you want and put it on the expense account. Just don't show it on the expense account."

So I travelled to the Caribbean (the British Virgin Islands), a $1,000-a-night resort in Fiji (this was in 1992, remember, when $1,000 was a lot for a single night) where Conrad Black went for his honeymoon, Bali, Adare Manor in Ireland, Thailand, Scotland, France, Morocco, Turks and Caicos, and France again.

As you might imagine, when I waltzed back into the *Toronto Sun* newsroom tanned and fit, I became the most hated journalist in Canada — with good reason.

While in the British Virgin Islands at Little Dix Bay, I met George and Irene Davis from Little Rock, Arkansas. George was the spitting image of the actor John Wayne and was known as The Duke. We met at a poolside dinner on what was our last evening at the resort. It was a very stuffy crowd, and we decided we were bored. I then shouted, "Let's change that!"

I stood up and, fully clothed, jumped into the pool. The Duke and Irene quickly followed. Within five minutes the entire resort was in the pool in their expensive attire, diamonds, Cartier watches, and all. It was no longer a boring evening.

Doug Creighton liked strong personalities as his columnists. And so arrived Barbara Amiel — beautiful, stylish, and with strong views on everything under the sun.

Doug soon had large ads throughout the paper. On top of photos of the two of us he put: FOTHERINGHAM & AMIEL. PAGE 12 WILL NEVER BE THE SAME. Innocent readers would never know there was more to it than that.

We were both single and divorced and had high energy. Short, hilarious lunches graduated to long dinners. We sensed the whole newsroom was smirking. We became "an item," even though I spent half my time in Vancouver. We were amused because of the fact that Barbara was Hard Right on everything while I tended to drift to the Left — as my annoyed readers always pointed out.

The Toronto Sun *ad announcing the arrival of Barbara Amiel and myself in the same newspaper.*

One day I got a call from Dona Harvey, managing editor of Vancouver's *Province* and an old friend. She invited me to a Saturday night dinner party at her home on the Simon Fraser University campus. I phoned Barbara, she flew out from Toronto, and we drove up to the top of Burnaby Mountain to SFU and arrived at the cocktail hour.

What I didn't know was that Dona had married William Klassen, a theology scholar. Half a dozen couples were in the living room, all of them connected with her husband's specialty. Barbara was in high spirits, wandering the room and introducing herself.

As the wine flowed, Barbara apparently wanted to display some Toronto brio to all these ignorant British California jerks. I heard a rising noise across the room where she was arguing with several chaps and shouting, "Fuck off!"

The wine continued to flow, and I was just going off to search for the men's loo when I heard a familiar female voice yell, "Cocksucker!" After I finished my business, I walked back to find the entire room empty except for Barbara. Everyone had fled into the kitchen and locked the door. We didn't even get dinner.

Time went on. I was always wandering around the world somewhere. Barbara, tired of her ex-sportswriter, moved on in search of a more major target. As we all know, she found it and in 1992 married Conrad Black, her fifth husband. I wrote a congratulatory column, listing her major accomplishments, including the one with her "colourful language" emptying an entire room in Vancouver.

She replied with an astonishing column in *Maclean's*, explaining that she knew for many years of Mr. Fotheringham's famed charm but had never once "dated him." This absolutely boggled the whole journalistic community in the country, not to mention half the MPs in Ottawa, where gossip gushes like water.

Even more incredible, she wrote that she had never even attended the dinner in Vancouver where her conversation had emptied the room. Fact checkers at *Maclean's* took what she said at face value and let the column run when all they had to do was make a simple phone call that would have revealed the inconsistencies.

Just before we are to be inducted into the Canadian News Hall of Fame, Conrad Black and I decide who will speak first. I did. He left.

I covered the first two weeks in 2007 of the trial in Chicago that sent Lord Conrad Black to prison. During the court breaks, Conrad came over to the press table and talked to me and the other Canadian reporters. Lady Amiel Black looked straight through me and pretended not to know who I was.

Conrad was released on a $2-million bond in 2010 to await a new trial. I tracked him down early in 2011 in New York to compliment him on one of his *National Post* columns. He replied with this email:

> Many thanks for your kind note. I will look forward to having a liquefied dinner with you when I have completed the rout of the American fascists. Our dear mutual friend Radler looks like a real champion, doesn't he? I'm just finishing my book about it all. I trust you have had a good summer and are well. All best to you and Anne.

Alas, his appeal was defeated and he was sent back to prison in September 2011. This means two things: (a) the liquefied dinner will be delayed again, and (b) His Highness will miss my book launch.

Such is life in the fast lane.

Once, at the end of the year, Doug Creighton took his senior department heads for lunch at Winston's where he had a table reserved every day, whether he showed up or not. As it happened, my son, Kip, was visiting me from Vancouver and I brought him along. Creighton called on each department head to give a year-end review of how they were doing. The circulation boss, the printing boss, et cetera, and he then came to the accountant.

The accountant said everything was okay with one exception. Fotheringham was $25,000 over on his expense account. "Well," said Creighton, "there's only one way to deal with that." At this stage my horrified son, not wanting to be present when his father was fired, excused himself and headed for the men's room. "The solution," said Creighton, "is to increase his expense account by $25,000."

In retrospect I think Doug enlisted me for his crazy ideas as a sort of surrogate for what he as a young reporter had wanted to do but couldn't anymore because he was tied down with too many corporate duties. A Freudian thought perhaps.

Here is one example of Doug's eccentricity and genius. He discovered a large Scottish immigrant in the press room and somehow heard him sing, perhaps in a pub or at a staff party. He was so impressed that, along with his friend Conrad Black, he took the young man out of the press room, bought him a wardrobe, and fixed him up with all the best agents. That's how John McDermott was discovered — now a major showbiz figure in Canada. John was in the hospital room with Doug's family when the newspaper man died. He also sang at Doug's funeral.

Once a year Doug mounted an expedition to an exotic spot, making sure he brought along a printer and his wife from the *Calgary Sun* (you can imagine their loyalty to him for the rest of their lives), an accountant and his wife from the *Ottawa Sun*, his own favourite secretaries, and a goof like me.

Another year he took us all to England and rented a famous castle (Clivedon) for the evening and had the Grenadier Guards march for us on the lawn while the band played. He made every other publisher in Canada look like a dolt.

All of this was part of his final demise when the bean counters finally got him. By this time, Maclean Hunter had bought the *Sun* and one day an executive from the company, armed with a lawyer, walked into Doug's office and told him he was being replaced. "Get out of my office!" Creighton roared. Then he phoned his wife. She was in her car, and he told her to pull over, not wanting to shock her. When she did so, he said, "We're going to New York tonight."

They flew to New York and went to their favourite restaurant when suddenly the door opened and in walked Ron Osborne, the very Maclean Hunter executive who had fired him earlier that day. Osborne took one look at Doug, turned, and fled.

As time passed, Doug developed Parkinson's disease. One day we had lunch and he said he wanted to do a small errand just up the way on Bloor

Street. I waited, then became a little worried when he didn't come back for some time. So I chased after him and found him going in the opposite direction. Doug wouldn't listen to me. He was a little out of it then. I had to phone his wife, terrified that I'd lost him. I told her that Doug had said he was going out to Woodbine Racetrack. His wife, Marilyn, said, "Don't worry. He does this almost every time he goes out now. He eventually winds up at home."

Years later I was back in Turks and Caicos with my new wife, Anne, when I saw on television that Creighton had died. I immediately phoned for a plane reservation the next day and flew to Toronto for the sad occasion. I had never changed my mind about a man as much in my life from my early thoughts of him as a lightweight cop shop reporter to becoming the most beloved employer in Canadian journalism where his staff would have died for him.

11
2000 Was a Busy Year

The year 2000 was a busy one. Having been to Antarctica for Christmas 1999, we left the ship in Ushuaia, Argentina, and were flown with the rest of the passengers to Santiago, Chile. We spent four lovely days there being entertained by Larry Lederman, the ambassador from Canada, and his wife, Patricia. To me Santiago was a smaller version of Buenos Aires — beautiful, with elegance and charm. It was a wonderful place to see in the new millennium.

We parted from the ship's passengers and crew in Santiago and made our way to Machu Picchu in Peru. Anne wanted to spend her birthday there. So, on January 6, we made our way by bus on a switchback road up the mountain to the site of this small city situated on top of the mountain. Being a westerner, I always praise the Rockies. But I have to admit, the Andes are more majestic and impressive. Hard to imagine but true. And with all of my travelling, I've never been to such a fascinating place.

It was ethereal, mystical, and interesting to walk through this city that had once boasted a population of a thousand people. How did they get the rocks up there to build the city? How did they know how to build a sophisticated irrigation system? What caused them to leave? So many curious, unanswered questions.

I was still sending my columns into *Maclean's*, which was a challenge when in places such as Machu Picchu. We stayed at the Machu Picchu Pueblo Hotel, but it didn't have a good hookup and the fax machine wasn't working. In those days I used a Tandy 200 computer, which had cups (reporters used to call them vaginas) that went over the phone receiver. However, no matter how I tried I couldn't get my column to go through. The deadline was fast approaching as was our train to return to Cuzco. Finally, in a panic, I called Bob Lewis, *Maclean's* editor. He said, "Just like the old days, Foth. Start dictating. I don't want to miss this column."

We made the train, returned to Cuzco, and went on to Lima, Peru. Next, the Amazon with pink dolphins, 4,500 species of butterflies, children in villages playing soccer, their pastime, and observing monkeys, piranha, and three-toed sloths. For us it was a wonderful experience … once.

Then it was back to Iquitos where we had originally started our journey into the heart of the Amazon headwaters. Although a city of 430,000, Iquitos is the largest city in the world whereby one can only get there by boat or plane. So we caught our flight to Lima and then the next day continued on to Miami where we stayed with our dear friends Allan and Emmanuelle Slaight on Fisher Island. A luxurious respite for multi-millionaires (Oprah Winfrey had a condo there at the time), it was a far cry from the Amazon.

A few days later, once we were home, I thought I had the flu or had maybe picked up a tropical bug. I got tested, but the doctors couldn't find anything wrong. They gave me a Valium and sent me home.

I felt well enough the next day and life carried on. We headed off to Santa Fe and Phoenix in Arizona and Palm Springs, California, continuing our journey following the trail of the tribes that had come across Alaska, through North America and Central America to settle in South America. The desert is a fascinating place — great scenery with chopped-off mountains and stunted growth. In Santa Fe at that time of year it was cool in the daytime but cold at night. However, it didn't deter us from going to art galleries, wandering the streets, and indulging Anne by buying a car coat made from an Indian blanket that she still gets complimented on to this day.

Leaving Santa Fe, we travelled to Phoenix where we visited my sister, Irene, and her husband, Don, who spend their winters in Arizona, both being from Vancouver. (Many Vancouverites spend their winters in this area of the southern United States.) Our day was full with picnics in the desert and other activities Irene arranged for our short but pleasant stay.

Next it was on to Palm Desert, a city next to Palm Springs, where we stayed with Jake and Judy Kerr, close friends from Vancouver. Jake was in the timber business at the time. A handsome man of about fifty-five with a wife equally as beautiful, they fitted the role of the perfect couple. They greeted us at the airport and took us in their vintage Rolls-Royce convertible (dark blue with beige interior) to their home in Morningside.

2000 Was a Busy Year

It had been a while since I was in Palm Springs area, having spent considerable time there when my children were growing up. Anne took an immediate liking to the place, and we both knew it was somewhere we'd come back to.

After a few days of golf and tennis, taking in the local colour, and eating fine food, Jake arranged a stretch limo to take all of us to Los Angeles, two and a half hours away. California was Jake's old stomping grounds, he having gone to university there. We went down memory lane with the two of them and enjoyed our time at the Belair where so many famous movie stars have stayed. But, of course, after two days we moved on to another saga of the journey. Jake and Judy returned to Palm Desert, while Anne and I picked up a black Camaro convertible (what else in Los Angeles?), drove along Sunset Boulevard, Bundy, Rockingham, and all the way out to Ocean Pacific Highway to Malibu to visit Norman and Dixie Jewison.

Norman is probably the best-known Canadian director of his time. *In the Heat of the Night, Moonstruck, The Russians Are Coming, The Russians Are Coming*, to name a few, were all directed by him. He owned a beach house (with neighbours such as Don Rickles), an apartment in New York City, a farm in Caledon, just outside Toronto, and skied at Klosters, Switzerland, every winter. Not bad for a poor boy who grew up in the Beach area of Toronto.

Our visit was just prior to Academy Awards time. One of Norman's movies, *The Hurricane* starring Denzel Washington as Rubin Carter, was up for an Oscar for best director and best male actor. Those were heady times. And staying with Norman brought home to me how political the Oscars are.

In the morning Norman was yelling on the phone to someone about how the powers that be were stirring up trouble, saying that his movie was based on a true story but wasn't accurate, hence not Oscar material. (Has anyone not heard of artistic licence?) Although Americans tend to overlook Canadian talent when it comes to the Oscars, they can't dismiss major hits such as *Titanic* and *Avatar*. Still, being a Canadian, Norman was perhaps at a disadvantage in getting the Oscar over an American director.

We left the day before the Oscars. In the end, neither Norman nor Denzel won an Academy Award. But our stay was quite enjoyable: sitting

My last time skiing was with Norman Jewison in Klosters, Switzerland. Norman, in his eighties, skis the black runs.

on Norman's patio overlooking the Pacific Ocean; going to Neptune's Seafood on the beach for lunch; dining at Spago in the evening.

Anne and I heard stories from Norman like the one in which Prime Minister Pierre Trudeau was holidaying in California. Norman was on the beach one day and saw a lonely couple there. He recognized Trudeau, who was with Margot Kidder, and not a bodyguard or Secret Service agent in sight. Apparently, Trudeau had lost his car keys. He was in a Speedo bathing suit and a towel and that was it. Norman asked him back to the house while they called to get another key for Trudeau's car rental. Norman told us how embarrassed he was when Dixie piped up to the prime minister, "Wash your feet free of sand before you go in the house."

He did.

The keys arrived, and off the romantic couple went. Hours later a driver appeared with an invitation to a black tie dinner the next evening with Trudeau. That's called gratitude.

After returning to Toronto, I didn't feel well again and had terrible pain. We went to a hospital emergency and had some tests done, but nothing was discovered. So I was given a Valium and sent home. When it happened again in June 2000, Anne said she wouldn't allow them to send me home until they found out what the problem was.

Numerous tests followed, and this time the doctors discovered I'd had a gallbladder attack. I was full of poison, which didn't allow them to operate. In fact, I was so full of poison, due to being sent home for the past six months, that it took six weeks of antibiotics to get rid of the poison and have an operation to remove the gallbladder.

In the meantime I'd been approached by Richard Addis, the new editor of the *Globe and Mail*, to join the paper. Richard was a young upper-crust divorced man about town from London's Fleet Street who was brought in by the Thomson family to clean shop at the paper and bring in fresh blood. My contract was coming up for renewal at *The Financial Post*, so I waited the appropriate length of time to hear if Sun Media was going to renew me. I heard nothing. So I asked Perry Goldsmith to contact the *Globe and Mail*. Once the contract was settled, I handed in my resignation to *The Financial Post*.

At this time my old buddy, Brian Mulroney, was the chairman of Sun Media. I received a call from him asking, "Foth, what's going on? What happened?" I explained that I waited the designated time and hadn't heard from them. So when approached by the *Globe* I'd decided to go. He was stunned, saying that I'd fallen through the cracks. After twelve years of service, I'd "fallen through the cracks." Go figure.

Later, I asked Richard Addis how he'd found out about me. He said he'd asked Jack Rabinovitch, the founder of the Giller Prize (the largest literary award for fiction in Canada), who was the best journalist to know who had an understanding of the pulse of the nation. Rabinovitch said, "There's only one. Dr. Foth."

Part of my deal with the *Globe and Mail* was to cover the Olympics in Sydney, Australia. I was to be there September 5, a few days before the opening ceremony. I now had two problems: accreditation for the Olympics and my gallbladder operation.

Due to being hired by the *Globe* and issues with my gallbladder, I was remiss in getting Olympic press accreditation. I had missed the deadlines for *Maclean's* and the *Globe* to get them for me and was on my own. So I called Dick Pound, a tall, imposing Montreal lawyer who was a big pooh-bah in the Olympic organization. I told him my predicament, and he said to leave it with him. Dick copied me on the emails sent to the Olympic headquarters. One from a young administrator read: "Who is Allan Fotheringham?"

Dick's reply: "Just do it!"

That's power. I got my accreditation.

Next was the gallbladder. I'd been scheduled to have the gallbladder operation on August 14. Normally, that wouldn't be a problem. These days a gallbladder takes forty-five minutes to remove by laparoscopic surgery. However, in my case, the procedure had been left so long that the short route was impossible.

Three and a half hours later Dr. Alexandra Easson, a young, very capable blonde, came out of the operating room and told Anne she didn't think I'd be going anywhere for at least six to eight weeks. My wife knew I had a history of bouncing back quickly. She told Dr. Easson we should see how things went. In the end, my wife made a deal with the doctor, saying she would take me to Bowen Island for three days at the end of August, and if I didn't do well, we'd come back to Toronto and not go to Australia. But if I did all right, we would go.

Fortunately, Jake and Judy Kerr had an extra home on Bowen Island off North Vancouver, which they offered to us for the three days. After lots of giggles with the Kerrs, we boarded a plane for Sydney, Australia, a long flight but not so bad when we were upgraded to executive class. Once there, though, I couldn't walk because my bad knee had swollen to the point that I couldn't put any weight on it.

So I got off the plane in a wheelchair and was put into a cab. When we got to the hotel, the doorman placed me in an office chair on wheels to get me to our room. I figured this would be a very long Olympics if I had to see it from a hotel room. Thank God there was a newsstand beside the hotel, along with a French bakery and a local café that could make my usual freshly squeezed orange juice in the morning.

With a good night's sleep under my belt, I woke up refreshed and with both legs ready to burn up the pavement at the Olympic Village. However, there was a phone message from Bob Lewis at *Maclean's*, saying a press release had been issued by one of Pierre Trudeau's sons to say he was very ill and had been sent home from the hospital. All of Trudeau's family had arrived, including Margaret, the mother of his children. Lewis wanted me to write a column on Trudeau for a special run of *Maclean's* that would be published if the former prime minister passed away.

That was one funeral I would have attended if I hadn't been at the other end of the world. Trudeau and I had had a lot of life together in a funny way, and I wanted to pay my respects to his family. So I wrote the column while Anne was out seeing the city with Catherine MacMillan, a chum from her university days who had recently moved to Sydney. Once again I had to struggle with getting a column out on a system that, in spite of the Olympics, wasn't as good as what I was used to. But success was mine.

Then the phone started ringing. The "troops" were in town. Matthew Fisher from the *Toronto Sun*, one of five sons of Doug Fisher, the "dean" of the Ottawa Press Gallery, made arrangements to meet Anne and me. Then Jack Cowin called, a Canadian who had lived in Australia for decades and had opened Kentucky Fried Chicken and Hungry Jack's franchises there. He invited us for drinks at his home in Point Piper. Jack was a close friend of Ed Lumley, who we had dined with at the Politics and the Pen dinner in Ottawa shortly before coming to Australia. It was Ed who had teamed us up with his old school chum in Australia.

Boy from Nowhere

Afterward we ran into former premier of Ontario David Peterson and his wife, Shelley, and arranged to have dinner with them. At the Olympic opening ceremonies we bumped into Stephen Richer, our buddy from the *Ocean Explorer* cruise to Antarctica. We also met Thomas Keneally, author of *Schindler's List*, and invited him and his daughter for lunch. Next it was tea with Lady Fairfax and then off to the Opera House to see George Shearing play piano with his band. We threw a party and invited Paul Henderson (president of the International Sailing Association) and his wife, Mary; Stephen Richer and three of his Aussie friends; Matthew Fisher; Andrew Phillips (*Maclean's* — Washington); James Deacon (*Maclean's* — Toronto); and Stefan Moore, son of Senator Janis Johnson, accompanied by his uncle, Jon Johnson. All of this *and* the Olympics!

It was my third Olympics, having covered the Calgary Games in 1988 and the Montreal edition in 1976. I wrote as much as was humanly possible and transmitted a column to the *Globe and Mail* every day as well as my weekly piece to *Maclean's*. News then came that Trudeau had died at 3:00 p.m. on September 28. The call came through to write another column.

By the time of the closing ceremonies, I had hit the wall. I was exhausted and sick of crowds. So Anne and I watched the closing ceremonies from a boat in the harbour, which allowed us to see everything and then take in the fireworks over Sydney Harbour Bridge. What a way to end an Olympic experience.

To avoid crowds at the airport, we remained in Sydney an extra day. During the Games, the city was vibrant — crowds everywhere and activities galore. But once they were over, it was business as usual. I couldn't believe how boring normal TV was in Australia. The coverage of the Games was so exceptional that I couldn't imagine we were in the same country. Obviously, the party was over.

After the Olympics, Anne and I went to Shanghai in China. I had been on a plane a few years before when a young man asked me when I'd last been to China. I said I'd been there with Canadian Secretary of State for External Affairs Mitchell Sharp on one of his missions. The young man said, "You call yourself a journalist and you haven't been to China in twenty-three years?" That small comment not only embarrassed me but stuck. So when Anne and I were in Australia I told her we had to go to China. The fact that it would take us eighteen hours to get there didn't deter me.

We had been to the handover of Hong Kong from Britain to China in 1997, but that wasn't mainland China. So we decided to visit Shanghai. Throughout history Hong Kong and Shanghai had had a feud of sorts with respect to financial and political power. Many capitalists and industrialists had left Hong Kong before the handover due to concern about communist rule. There was a general feeling that the shift in power would divert back to the mainland in the direction of Shanghai after all those decades. Upon our arrival, it seemed that speculation had borne fruit. The city was changing so rapidly that one-third of the world's construction cranes were in Shanghai.

Our sojourn in Shanghai was more than pleasant. A week-long holiday had been declared. What luck! Everything was open except the factories, which meant we had blue skies and no smog. We spent time with the Canadian consul general, a forty-five year-old man named Stewart Beck, who brought us up-to-date with what was going on in China and what it meant for Canada. In fact, Prime Minister Jean Chrétien was arriving on October 21 on a trade mission. We would miss him by two weeks. Never mind, I assured the consul general, the prime minister would be fine without me.

We did the usual touristy things, enjoyed the art deco, and bought coats and suits made in forty-eight hours. Then we flew to Xian to view the terra cotta warriors. They were only a one-and-a-half-hour flight from Shanghai. Anne, with her art background and interest in all things old (including me), was determined to see the impressive mausoleum that had taken seven hundred thousand men to build. I was glad she had dragged me there before our return trip back to Canada.

12
Conquering Africa

This father, as a tadpole, was fascinated with Richard Halliburton and his derring-do. Halliburton was an American explorer and writer who dazzled small boys with his dashing adventures. In 1922 he made an expedition to mysterious Tibet. He traced on foot Hernán Cortés's route in the conquest of Mexico. He travelled around the world in his own plane in 1931–32.

Halliburton also traced the route of the first Crusade and the travels of Alexander the Great in the conquest of Asia. He followed the trail of Hannibal from Carthage to Italy. He swam the locks of the Panama Canal. When this father was young, he wanted to be Richard Halliburton — who was lost at sea in a typhoon while trying to sail in a Chinese junk from Hong Kong to San Francisco in 1939.

While Halliburton was a voyeur, Cecil Rhodes was a doer. The old colonial bully hit it rich in the diamond fields around Kimberley in what is now South Africa. Before he was thirty, he personally controlled at one point some 90 percent of the world's diamond output. The Rhodes Scholarships, of course, still bear his name as once did Rhodesia. Rhodes had a grandiose vision of "a map red (i.e., British) from Cape to Cairo." He set out to build the Cape-to-Cairo railway but didn't quite make it, being busy with the Boer War, among other things.

So, father has this son. Son with his usual luck wins, as a door prize at the St. Andrew's Annual Ball in Vancouver, an Air Canada ticket that can take him as far as Athens, Greece. Father and son hatch this idea. While father goes to Cape Town to free Nelson Mandela and then head north, son will go to Cairo and head south. They will attempt to do what Cecil Rhodes failed to do: link the Cape to Cairo.

Son arrives in the cradle of democracy and immediately hikes up the Acropolis to view the Parthenon. It is covered with scaffolding from a Japanese construction crew. Father, at a rally celebrating Mandela's release from twenty-seven years in prison, eager to be a reporter again, rushes in where only fools tread and finds himself caught between police bullets and rioters' hurled bottles. Father decides to go back immediately to being a thumb-sucking columnist in an office.

When Son meets a Greek who wants to sail across the Mediterranean in a small boat, they realize they need a third person to help man the twenty-four-hour watch and find a young Tokyo lawyer who testifies to his sailing skills. Once afloat, it turns out the Japanese man has never been on water before. He throws up steadily for four days. When they reach Egypt, the Japanese fellow has lost eleven pounds.

Father, with the aid of a cable car, marches to the top of Table Mountain. It is 3,763 miles west to Rio de Janeiro, 7,927 miles to Montreal, 6,009 miles north to London, 6,837 miles south to Sydney, and 8,044 miles to Beijing. The memorial to Cecil Rhodes overlooks the University of Cape Town, whose students now use it as a trysting spot. It faces north — to Cairo.

There is a communications problem on the Dark Continent. Because of the political situation, African stations allow no telephone service with boycotted South Africa. Son can't find father; father has no idea where son is. So son phones a lady in Vancouver who phones father in South Africa — at considerable cost to the treasury. It is a shaky source of information, only one step up from jungle drums.

Son apparently is on the Sinai Peninsula, south of Israel. In return for room and board he is teaching English to camel drivers huddled at his feet in the dust. He stops short of Shakespeare. Father, having freed Mandela, spends his time arguing with telephone operators that there must be some way, in 1990, to reach a hotel, any hotel, in far-off Kenya.

Travelling up the Nile, Son reaches the fabled ruins of Luxor and discovers the ineffable sensations of eating deep-fried pigeon, which is apparently short on drumsticks. Father notices, on the way to the Cape Town airport, an overpass decorated with new spray-painted graffiti: PREPARE AND PLAN NOW — TO GOVERN.

Son is thirty-six hours on an Egyptian train in third class, with chickens and the lot. Some of the passengers sleep in the luggage racks. Unfortunately, the chickens with them are awake. And doing what chickens do. Son alights after thirty-six hours, his hair full of delightful chicken droppings. Character-building. It's good for a son. Meanwhile Father has made it north to Zimbabwe, tracing Cecil's railway all the way to the hardship surroundings of the Victoria Falls Hotel.

With the Vancouver telephone exchange now the hub (and profit centre) of the world, it is determined that Nairobi in Kenya shall be the rendezvous. Son, on his arrival at his usual $2.50-a-night hostelry, feels it only proper to get spruced up to meet father — and a hotel with the first hot shower in a month. A haircut would be wise. "We have a little problem here," says the lady barber. Dandruff? "No, lice." It costs 50 cents for the trim, $20 for the hospital visit.

And so as the sun sets over yet another country that used to be British red on the map, son looks longingly at father's modern hot shower, the pot at the end of the rainbow. But he can't touch it, since the delousing powder must do its fearsome work for two days. It's character-building, I tell you.

Father and number two son, Kip, the one foraging south on stout shoe leather and street smarts, the other struggling north on an expense account, meet in the middle of Africa, right on the equator. Father meets son. Stanley finds Livingstone. Rest easy, Cecil Rhodes, we have finally done Cape to Cairo.

13
Me and Mulroney

You have to realize that I invented Brian Mulroney.

The second column I ever wrote for *Maclean's* coincided with Robert Standstill's announcement that three straight electoral defeats by Pierre Elliott Himself were enough. And he asked the Regressive Convertible Party to mount a leadership convention in Ottawa in February 1976 to pick a successor.

I assayed the obvious candidates and advised that Jack Horner was too stupid and Paul Hellyer was too stubborn and Joe Clark was too young and yada-yada. If the Tories had any brains, I advised — as they had shown they hadn't — they would figure out that the reason they had been shut out of power in Ottawa for most of the century was that they could never break into Quebec.

Why not, I suggested, take a flyer on someone I had never met but had been keeping an eye on from afar. Name of Brian Mulroney, fluently bilingual, good record as a prominent Montreal lawyer who had achieved television attention as a star on the Cliché Commission of Inquiry into Union Corruption.

He came with a beautiful young wife whose prominent father, Dimitrije Pivnicki, originally from Sarajevo, Yugoslavia, was the psychiatrist who had accepted Margaret Trudeau into his hospital's care and, after she left on her own accord, observed that there was a young lady who needed a lot of help.

Two weeks later my secretary at the *Vancouver Sun* buzzed and said, "Allan, there's a Mr. Mulroney on the phone from Montreal."

I picked up the receiver and didn't even say hello. "When did you decide to run?"

The deep baritone at the other end of the line said, "The second time I read it in your column."

That was the start of an interesting relationship that really hasn't been resolved to this day.

Mulroney said he would be coming to Vancouver in several weeks for the usual "fact-finding mission" to see if he would run for the leadership. He suggested we have a drink when he arrived. Certainly, I replied, by this time having dubbed him in my column the Candidate from Whimsy, since he was my own invention. He loved it, for years after announcing, "This is Whimsy," when I answered the phone.

The day he arrived on the Wet Coast he invited me to Hotel Vancouver. In a lavish suite he was surrounded by buddies from Montreal and acolytes. A waiter approached and asked for our drink orders. The Jaw That Walked Like a Man paused a little too long and said, "I think I'll have a beer." That struck me instantly as wrong, trying to impress, and I ordered my usual gin *mit* tonic.

We talked for about ten minutes, the acolytes as always chewing the drapes, and I remember thinking, *Is that all there is?* — to borrow the title of the old Peggy Lee song. *Is this the future prime minister I've invented? All Irish charm and bullshit?* Being Irish myself — despite my stepfather's surname — I recognized it immediately.

Brian certainly had street smarts (now corporate smarts). On his way to the top (he lost the Conservative leadership race in 1976 but won in 1983 before becoming prime minister from 1984 to 1993), he figured the most practical thing to do was to get an influential journalist who had a national audience in his hip pocket. For a while he thought it was Peter C. Newman (as Conrad Black once did until Conrad read the Newman book that was based on open access to the formidable Black brain ... and mouth).

So it was that I became the teacher's pet at 24 Sussex Drive. There for all the banquets, all the parties, and in time became a great friend of Mila, who could work a room better than anyone I'd ever seen. When the PM was travelling out of town, Mila and I often dined alone, sharing the gossip that was and is Ottawa's main industry.

I was a close friend of Pierrette Lucas, Mila's attractive and witty press secretary, and we were well acquainted with Harrington Lake, the prime ministerial weekend retreat in the Gatineau Hills north of Ottawa that featured a huge, manicured lawn. One year, on their wedding anniversary, Pierrette and I gave Brian and Mila a huge wooden croquet set to put the lawn to work.

Ronald Reagan was tall, but I'm taller.

One day Southam bureau chief Charlie Lynch, the dean of the Ottawa Press Gallery, took me aside for a chat. He said that I obviously had a great journalistic career ahead of me, but all the chatter among the regulars at the gallery bar was that I was ruining my objectivity — and therefore reputation — by being so close to the Mulroneys.

Boy from Nowhere

The moment seemed judicious to accept the offer of Southam News to move to Washington for a five-year gig to "launder myself" from a too-close association to someone I had supposedly invented. This became assuredly clear when one Sunday morning at the guest cottage up the shore of Harrington Lake there arrived by speedboat a waiter with eggs Benedict, smoked salmon, and a tall bottle of champagne for Pierrette and me. Charlie Lynch was right. Washington and Ronnie Reagan, I realized, awaited.

When I arrived back in the Ottawa Press Gallery in 1990 — "cleansed," as it were — I treated the prime minister with my usual rough and objective criticism as he deserved. One day a gallery veteran asked Mulroney what he thought of my column. The prime minister replied, "Piss on Fotheringham." More columns followed. Mila took a mallet from the croquet set, wrapped it up, and mailed it to my employer with a note enclosed: "Please tell Mr. Fotheringham to stick this up his yazoo." The friendship ended.

Years went by. A decade passed. Brian Mulroney was in dark seclusion in Baie-Comeau, Quebec, his entire life reputation shattered by revelations of accepting $225,000 in $1,000 bills from the despicable Karlheinz Schreiber.

One day I checked into St. Michael's Hospital in Toronto for a routine four-hour colonoscopy. Thanks to incredible medical incompetence, I was there for five months.

While I was in the hospital, my seventy-fifth birthday arrived. So did a phone call. The famed Mulroney Rolodex was still operating. He had heard I was in trouble and had tracked me down to offer me warm and sincere birthday wishes.

The Irish blood flows thicker than water.

14
Pierre Elliott Himself

On Pierre Elliott Trudeau's first foray into British Columbia to divine whether he had support for his whimsical bid for the Liberal leadership in 1968, his backers scheduled a Sunday evening reception at Hotel Vancouver's main ballroom. As he was upstairs changing his clothes, an expectant crowd waited for the ballroom doors to be opened.

I was there, and standing first in line was a vibrantly beautiful young redhead. She was literally jumping up and down, asking her female companion, "Do you think he'll remember me?" Mr. Trudeau came down and fought his way through the crowd. She threw herself at him, and yes, he definitely did remember her. It was their first meeting since he'd met her in a bikini in Tahiti.

I was in the *Vancouver Sun* newsroom early one morning in 1971 when the spectacular news came over the teletype that the professional bachelor Pierre Trudeau at age fifty-one was going to marry twenty-two-year-old Margaret Sinclair. I knew her father well, since Jimmy Sinclair as the fisheries minister in the Trudeau cabinet was the senior Liberal MP in British Columbia and we often shared a drink.

Getting into my car, I raced across Lions Gate Bridge to the Sinclair home in West Vancouver. It was 10:00 a.m., the first bottle of champagne was just popping, and Mrs. Sinclair had a story. Margaret had phoned a week earlier to announce that the prime minister had just proposed, but of course it had to be kept quiet until the official announcement. When in Vancouver, Jimmy dined every day at the exclusive (males only) Vancouver Club where all the city's business tycoons drank their lunch five days a week.

Margaret's mother announced to her husband that he wasn't allowed to have a single drink with his companions for a week, lest the secret slip out through the gin. Jimmy, by now filled to the gills with Canada Dry ginger ale, opened another bottle of the bubbly. We were just getting into the hard stuff, Mrs. Sinclair off in the kitchen, and he said, "Allan, I have five beautiful daughters. Why would he pick the dumb one?"

Well, as it happens, in November 2010 the "dumb one" had her third book, *Changing My Mind*, at the number one spot on the *Maclean's* bestseller list. In the previous two books she told how her husband loved his three sons and — slyly detecting which trees have rotting trunks — proved to his adoring tadpoles that he could fell a tree with a single kick. Concluded Margaret before marriage: "he was destined for eternal solitude."

The millionaire who "inherited his mother's Puritanism and frugality" insisted at 24 Sussex Drive on "drying himself with the smallest and meanest towel he could lay his hands on." This superb athlete wouldn't "play a single competitive game." Did he dream in French or English? He said, patiently as if to a child, "I don't think in words, Margaret. I think in the abstract."

There was, chillingly, the discussion on the FLQ crisis with the PM supposedly explaining to his wife that if ever she or any baby of hers was kidnapped there would be no deal, no amnesty. Would that mean he would allow her and her children to be killed? If we are to believe Margaret, the stern answer was: "Yes. Yes, I would." And there was the shock of the pitifully innocent (not in the biblical sense, thank you) bride discovering that the cerebral Trudeau didn't exchange presents at Christmas.

Then there was the husband who arrived home "punctually" at 6:45 every night, swam "forty-four laps, never more, never less," and seventeen minutes later was ready for his sons and then dinner "precisely at eight," followed by forty-five minutes during which he would do nothing requiring deep thought while he "as he puts it, digests." Margaret added: "I was absolutely forbidden to interrupt him as he worked. Time with Wifey was over."

That sounds like downtown Etobicoke.

Trudeau's long-time friend and confident, Gérard Pelletier, once explained that while Pierre gave the impression of a daring risk-taker, he was, in fact, a most cautious person. (His long delay in risking the perilous shores of marriage, if nothing else, proved that.) Pelletier pointed out that Trudeau would launch his canoe over an apparent stretch of whitewater, but only after charting and checking beforehand on foot every bit of the route. He took risks, said Pelletier, but only carefully calculated ones. In fact, little was left to chance. "Reason over passion" was the family motto.

Pierre Elliott Himself

His whole record of serving us (1968 to 1979, 1980 to 1984) confirms a confession he once made at an Ontario Liberal conference in Kingston: "I personally get a fair amount of pleasure from daring people to do certain things. That is why I'm enjoying this period in my political life." He was an emotional roller coaster, dozing between fits of passion. The economy always bored him. He lunged at it only in fits of exasperation. The War Measures Act was his finest hour, bringing out a courageous, tough leader who rallied the nation against an unknown foe with his chilling eloquence and undeniable courage. Trudeau for once was roused, and he responded magnificently.

He needed confrontation to concentrate his frozen-in-aspic intellect. The boy in Saskatchewan tossing wheat at him was told he was about to get his ass kicked. The demonstrator in Vancouver was cuffed. The striking mail truck drivers from Montreal were told what edifying diet they could eat as the PM of all the people sped off in his limousine. The TV reporter on the Parliament steps who pressed him on how far he would go in restricting civil liberties in the FLQ drama was told: "Just watch me." Watch me, if you think you can kick sand in my face, just watch me.

Pierre Trudeau, in essence, never outgrew the need to be the youth, knotted bandana around his neck, running before the bulls of Pamplona. He liked daring to do certain things: the first to wear sandals and an ascot in Parliament; to throw snowballs at Lenin's statue in Moscow; to ride around Montreal on a motorcycle wearing a German helmet; to marry a dazzling beauty thirty years his junior; to be the first prime minister to tell an MP to "fuck off" in the House of Commons; to do a mocking pirouette behind a queen. Always there was the image of the little boy wanting to stick his tongue out during the formal photography session.

The man of masks who told biographer George Radwanski that he was so sickly and insecure as a child that he purposely set out to build a physique and a steel will that would repel all outsiders wobbled between the arrogance seen by the public and the shyness seen by his intimates.

Back in the days when he still spoke to your blushing agent, he once confided to my notebook that the toughest thing to master in his early years as prime minister was learning to be a team player. As a loner who would never touch team sports as a youth and preferred to test his body in single combat with the elements, he suddenly found himself part of a team — thirty or so bodies sitting around a Cabinet table — and he had to think as a team player. It wasn't easy, he confessed, to wipe out all the solitary mental attitudes developed over his life. As a grown man, he had to re-educate himself.

Tom Axworthy, one of the guests at Trudeau's eightieth birthday party in 1999 at Jean Chrétien's home at 24 Sussex Drive, used to dine out on the stories of the lofty one's famed disinclination to remember the names of even his top aides in the Prime Minister's Office.

"I'd been there for two years," Axworthy recalled, "and whenever he wanted to talk to me he would just say, 'Get me the fat guy.'"

Paul Manning was a speechwriter in the PMO when Trudeau, his popularity waning, was facing his third election campaign. Ushered into the prime minister's presence, Manning suggested he had a bright idea for Trudeau's address the next day to the steelworkers' union in Hamilton. It was that even Hank Aaron, who at the time was chasing Babe Ruth's all-time home run record, having whiffed once and whiffed twice, still had a chance with a third strike.

Trudeau: "Who's Hank Aaron?"

Pierre Trudeau and I solving the problems of the world. Courtesy of the *Vancouver Sun.*

Manning, clearing his throat, explained that Aaron was the baseball player who was about to break Babe Ruth's home run record.

Trudeau: "Who's Babe Ruth?"

By now sweating nervously, Manning explained that Babe Ruth was the most famous baseball player in history. Trudeau, finally getting the three-strike analogy, thought it was a good idea. So next day before the doubting steelworkers the PM allowed that perhaps he hadn't been perfect in his first two terms but deserved a third try. "Even Hank Aaron gets a third strike. And you all know who he is — the guy who's going to break the home run record of Baby Ruth!"

Trudeau went through two periods in his life. First, he was a brilliant loner who walked through life according to his own rules. Then he was someone casually thrust into power — almost against his own will — who came to enjoy the power very much.

As the emotional reactions to Trudeau's passing washed in, it was remembered that his contemporary as a leader when he first took power was Charles de Gaulle. Lyndon Baines Johnson, we tend to forget, was president when Trudeau was prime minister. The Americans went through four presidents during Trudeau's first tenure. The British picked five prime ministers in the same time.

He gave Canada, always the wallflower at the North American dance, something it never had before: a belief and lusty pride that we had a guy we could stack up against anyone in the world.

In 1968, still riding the euphoria of Montreal's Expo 67, we suddenly discovered this reluctant warrior, who confessed to the press that he at first thought it "a joke" that he, of the Three Wise Men brought in from Quebec by Pearson, would be considered a prime-ministerial candidate. But there he was — rich, casual, witty, attracted to attractive women. Furthermore, he was athletic and effortlessly bilingual!

Lester Pearson, who couldn't really speak French but could fake it well enough for formal occasions, predicted that after he left 24 Sussex Drive there would never be another Canadian prime minister who wasn't completely bilingual. He was right, of course, and Trudeau's official bilingualism legislation ensured that. The proof (and the victims) of that were John Crosbie and Preston Manning, each in his own time arguably the most intelligent MP in the Commons.

Boy from Nowhere

The most poignant moment of Trudeau's successful return in the 1980 campaign came one night in a high school in, of all unlikely Tory places, Prince Albert, Saskatchewan. A tired Pierre Trudeau stood on a stage while a choir of more than a dozen young boys launched into "O Canada."

But the boys launched into "O Canada" in French, and once Trudeau realized what was happening, it was almost impossible to describe the look that spread over his face. In all my years of watching the moody man, I had never seen such obvious joy on his face.

Here in the home of "unhyphenated Canadianism" was the proof that it could be done — this inflexible man's dream of portable bilingualism. Beaming (and Pierre Trudeau didn't beam easily) as the anthem soared forth in his own language, the country's most famous single parent gazed fondly at the younger boys who were about the same age as the three he had left at home.

I used to travel the world with Trudeau on his campaign plane. Your humble scribe, one night after a G7 meeting in Rome, was smuggled into a party thrown for Trudeau by Roloff Beny, the famed Alberta photographer. It was midnight under the moon on a rooftop garden overlooking the Tiber River. Exotic people of all three sexes floated about, serving champagne and smoked salmon.

Trudeau walked in and, in semi-disgust, said, "Oh, Fotheringham, you remind me of Cyrano de Bergerac. You make enemies so easily." And he launched into a long quotation — in French, of course.

"Oh, Mr. Trudeau," I said, "I wouldn't know what you're talking about, naturally, since I'm from western Canada."

He turned on his heel and walked off. We didn't talk again for two years.

In essence, the Ottawa Press Gallery was afraid of Trudeau, intimidated by his intellect, wary of his withering wit. He pretended, of course, never to read the press. In our long encounters he gave me three compliments, two of which he was unaware.

The first time I was ever in Ottawa from my Vancouver retreat was at a press conference where he instructed, at the finish, that all the press should leave so he could talk to his caucus. Since no one knew me, in the daring stupidity that marked my young life, I decided to hide behind the drapes. Several attendants, of course, detected me and loudly frog-marched me out.

Pierre and Margaret were standing on the stage, watching all this, and Pierre asked, "What's all that fuss about?"

"He's a reporter," Margaret explained.

She told me later that her husband's reply was: "That's funny. He doesn't dress like one."

Once I became an Ottawa regular, when Trudeau finished his press conferences, he would push through the scribes on the way to his limo and punch me in the stomach, an indication he had read my column that morning and didn't like it.

On the June morning in 1984 when he left politics, he dusted off his white Mercedes-Benz convertible and rolled up the long driveway at Rideau Hall to deliver his resignation to the governor general. The press mob, of course, was there. I was out front, and as he eased to a stop, he twisted his wheel at the last moment and ran over my foot. I took it as the final compliment.

When Trudeau's son drowned, I sent him a personal note, father to father. Reporters aren't supposed to write to politicians. I guess that's why he was different.

15
The Reluctant Queen

In all the recent fuss over the sixtieth anniversary of Queen Elizabeth II on the throne of a foreign country, there are two myths floating out there in the void. One is that Dr. Foth, who thinks the Brits should stick with their royalty and that Canada should grow up, knows nothing about the Royals. That isn't true.

The second is the misconception that Good Queen Bess is stubbornly sticking to her crown and selfishly won't give it up to the resolutely under-employed Prince Charles. Both beliefs are mistaken. I am here to disabuse you of them.

In 1981 your agent, for his sins, was ordered to cover the Cinderella wedding of the Virgin Di and the chap with the large ears. I sat some fifty feet from the fairy-tale ceremonies in St. Paul's Cathedral and was struck most of all by one overriding image: the glum and sorrowful look on the face of the mother of the bridegroom.

One would have thought — all London aflame with a party passion understandable in a people who lead such dreary lives — that the queen would have been beaming with pride. She wasn't. She looked unhappy. We have shared a glass or two at off-the-record press receptions on the royal yacht and, at the time, your blushing republican was struck by (a) her daintiness, (b) the fact she is more attractive in person than in pictures, and (c) her understated wit that bordered on withering.

Implicit in that was good humour. The good humour had disappeared by the time of St. Paul's Cathedral. She has never smiled since. The reason she has never smiled since is because, as she gazed at the altar and the fairy-tale wedding, she knew within herself that her son would probably be an old and tired and discouraged man before he ever acceded to the throne she would like to give up.

She would like to, but she has decided she can't. Because of the past and the conduct of her offspring, she has been advised by her

Buckingham Palace advisers that she has to stay, for the survival of the monarchy.

The past, of course, was her selfish uncle, Edward, Prince of Wales, who abandoned the throne for the conniving and much-married Wallis Simpson (an American!) and spent the rest of his life wandering in exile, a pitiful figure. Good Queen Bess can never forgive Uncle Edward for that: the abdication forced her shy father, who didn't want the job, to become king (subject of the 2010 award-winning movie *The King's Speech*) — a task that killed him and therefore ruined the youth of a twenty-five-year-old bride who had to accept a heavy crown.

If King Edward VIII could junk the job for love, can Elizabeth now do it because she is old? And wants her long-impatient son to have it? Nope. The dangerous precedent can't be repeated. It's too fragile a myth as it is. The crown isn't something you can abandon, willy-nilly, as the coinage would be debased. It's not a job, it's a calling — a lifetime one.

Little wonder the moody Prince Charles was reduced to talking to flowers and wandering the Scottish woods in his kilt while the wife who upstaged him flew off to the disco with Sarah Ferguson. His mother turned eighty-five in 2011 and certainly isn't infirm. The genes are in the family. The Queen Mum went past a hundred and was still going strong with the pearls, the corgis, and the gin.

The Brits are used to longevity. George III stuck it out for fifty-nine years on the throne. Queen Victoria did better, lasting almost sixty-four. The incumbent may beat that. No wonder she looks so glum. No wonder Prince Charles is reduced to complaining about architecture.

There is the additional problem of the progeny. The Royals were once a tight little family unit. Now there are so many of them that some, inevitably one supposes, will fall off the back of the truck. Divorce has entered the fairy tale, through Princess Margaret, Prince Charles, Prince Andrew, and Princess Anne, her husband, Mark Phillips, having been in a paternity suit in New Zealand with some horsey lady, and Lord Snowdon, Margaret's former husband, in a similar pickle.

Fleet Street warned that some of the juvenile antics threatened to bring the Windsors down to the level of the partying Eurotrash aristocrats. There was Randy Andy with his porn star, Koo Stark. Fergie, with her aggressive bad taste in clothes, seemed a grenade about to explode in the tabloids any week. And she did with the sucking-toes incident while topless. There was always some stray cousin up for speeding or drugs or both.

Does anyone deserve to be stuck with one job beyond fifty-nine years? Nope. But those are the breaks. It's not a job; it's an inheritance. Duty calls. In order to fulfill the duty — and keep the myth alive — Elizabeth must watch her one reliable son grow old from misuse and brood from inactivity.

She knows the secret to his morose nature and how to lift it: hand him the crown. But she can't, won't, because it would destroy the myth. It's all high-class soap opera, and the British public loves to watch (while Canada is trying to grow up without it).

Prince Charles has fallen off a polo pony once too often and has been advised to give up the sport. What to do? Perhaps he could try reading the encyclopedia from front to back, as bored Governor General Ed Schreyer once tried in Rideau Hall. Or write down what flowers say when they talk back. I'm only offering advice. It's going to be a long wait. Might as well wait with your former mistress, Camilla, by your side, now married and queen-in-waiting.

On the last day of August 1997, I was celebrating my birthday with my children on Bowen Island off Vancouver, when my daughter, Francesca, pulled me off the dance floor to tell me the dreadful news that Lady Di and Dodi had been killed in a car crash in France. My future bride, Anne Libby, calmly said, "That will be the biggest news story in the world for the next week. You were at her wedding. You should be at her funeral."

I sprinted to a bank machine, raced to Vancouver's airport, flew over the North Pole to London, and immediately phoned *Maclean's* editor Bob Lewis in Toronto and asked him what he thought of me possibly going to the funeral. He said he would think about it, then asked, "Where are you?"

"Heathrow Airport," I replied.

"Oh."

That's why Robert Lewis is a perfect example of a fine editor. And as Camilla Parker Bowles hid in the wings, Britain buried "England's Rose" while the world watched.

16
I Meet the Gem

I tell people that I was married for seventeen years and then was a "lonely bachelor" for seventeen more.

But that's not quite true. I did have the odd date along the way. I was almost engaged a couple of times, which didn't work out, and I also heard through the grapevine that I was getting married a few times I wasn't aware of. I was the last to know. But all of that changed when I met the Gem.

In 1993 I was at a birthday party for Zoe Band, the daughter of Sarah Band, a friend of mine, when I noticed a strikingly beautiful woman standing alone in the corner. (She later told me she was jet-lagged.) I asked someone and got her name. The next day I called Sarah and asked, "Who is Anne Libby?"

Sarah said, "Anne Libby is not only my closest friend, but she's the best-kept secret in Toronto."

I immediately took note and decided I should take Anne to lunch.

As it turned out, Anne was an art gallery owner whose gallery was located near the *Toronto Sun*. One day while walking back from Biagio on King Street East where I'd had a leisurely lunch I walked into a gallery and asked to see Anne.

"Anne? There is no 'Anne' here," I was told.

"Yes, there is," I said. "She owns the place."

"No," the employee said. "Susan's the owner."

So much for my luncheon date.

A year later we were both at the same birthday party. I mentioned to Anne that I'd gone into her gallery and was told someone named Susan was the owner. After asking a couple of questions (and suggesting jokingly that perhaps I took Susan out for the rest of the year), Anne explained that her gallery wasn't between Biagio and the *Toronto Sun*. It was east of the *Sun*'s building.

"There isn't anything east of the *Sun*'s building," I replied.

"Yes, there is," she said. *"Me."*

I wasn't going to let another year go by without having lunch with this intriguing woman. A date was set for La Maquette, a romantic French restaurant also on King Street East.

The day prior to my luncheon with Anne I had a photo shoot set up by photographer Beverley Rockett. She suggested a series of photos showing the "Ladies Who Lunch with Dr. Foth." The photo shoot was to occur at the end of Shaftesbury Avenue where there was a bronze sculpture of a bench and a young couple seated on it. The ladies were to sit with me on the bench one at a time beside the bronze couple.

Beverley had a schedule detailing when each lady would show up: Adrienne Clarkson, 9:30 a.m.; Pamela Wallin, 10:00 a.m.; Catherine Nugent, 10:30 a.m.; Popsy Johnstone, 11:00 a.m.; Geills Turner, 11:30 a.m.; Anna Porter, noon. Twenty-one in total. It was a long, fun-filled day. In the end, Beverley sold the photo spread to *Toronto Life*. It ran around the same time as another piece in a different magazine, stating that I knew how women should dress.

The next day Anne and I met at my usual lunchtime: 12:12 p.m. Over the second drink, I found out she was forty-two years of age. (There is a saying that states a European woman will tell you her weight but never her age. A North American woman will tell you her age but never her weight.)

Apparently, I had met Anne previously in 1991 at a dinner party at the home of interior designer Maureen Milne. Anne says she obviously didn't make an impression on me, since I sat beside her and said about two sentences to her all night. I could deny this meeting except she has the photo to prove it. I think it was more jet lag on my part, having just returned from one of the ten best resorts of the world (or at least that was my excuse).

She then told me she had never been married. Ever the smartass, I asked, "You mean you've never been proposed to?"

Her answer was: "Yes, seven and three-quarter times." She thought this would throw me off.

It didn't. It intrigued me. I've never once in our relationship asked her about the seven. Every woman has secrets that must remain intact. But I'm curious, fascinated, to this day about the three-quarters.

Another question. "Would you have had your picture taken yesterday as one of the ladies who lunch with Dr. Foth?"

Her answer: *"No."*

We started seeing each other on a regular basis, and the following May we went to Portugal. It was the first of a number of trips that would take us to twenty-six countries over the next seven years, not including returning to a number of them during that time.

Anne has a passion for travel that equals mine — Ireland, Italy, France, China, Bali, Australia, Peru, Chile, Argentina, the Philippines, to name a few. We went to the Hong Kong handover in 1997, a cremation of one of the kings of Bali, and Antarctica for the millennium. We are happier flying somewhere than being at home.

Travelling leads to adventure, meeting new people, and having new experiences. It also adds to the number of countries I've been to, which allows me to have a subtitle on my memoirs that indicates I've been to ninety-one countries.

Anne, I found out quickly, had a withering wit that kept me on my toes and, when needed, put me back on my heels. Her business degree from the University of Toronto was the perfect fit with a career opposite — a tender poet who couldn't understand a bank account if it fell on him.

She wasn't intimidated by my headline friends who tried to intimidate her. And they couldn't understand how I could be so lucky to find her after my seventeen years of bad behaviour.

Around year three we started discussing marriage. I had always wanted to remarry, even though I'd been labelled a ladies' man. She was beautiful, bright, and sophisticated, and my kids loved her. And, more important, I loved her. I arranged for a ring and prepared a trip to New York City for Valentine's Day.

It was a beautiful day in New York. We had asked Liz Turner (daughter of former Prime Minister John Turner) for lunch, since she was living in New York City at the time. After a leisurely lunch of swapping lies and gossip, we bid her adieu. I then asked Anne if she wanted to go to the Pierre for a drink. When we arrived in the hotel bar, it wasn't busy. I ordered a bottle of champagne. There was a single rose in the vase on the table, and with two glasses of champagne just poured, I got down on bended knee (my good knee) and presented the ring. Holding back tears, I asked her to marry me. Fortunately for me, she said, "Yes." But as we sipped champagne, I started to tear up. Anne wanted to know what was wrong. I explained that I actually wanted to propose at the Plaza Hotel. "Well, you will then."

Off we went over the square to the Plaza. As we arrived, it was apparent they were between lunchtime and tea time. The blue-rinse ladies were lined up waiting for tea. I went to enter, thinking we could get a drink before tea when the maître d' said to me, "Sir, you'll have to wait for tea. It's $75."

Astonished, I whispered to him, "I'm trying to propose to this lady." "In that case, sir, that will be $15. Right this way."

He arranged for drinks, and with tears welling in my eyes, I got down again on bended knee and asked if Anne would marry me.

As I presented her with the engagement ring for the second time, we heard a huge sigh from all the blue-rinse ladies in the lineup. For them it was worth $75 to be there and witness this romantic moment. Valentine's Day will never be the same, not for us, not for them.

We quickly determined that it would be impossible to have a traditional wedding. My mother was elderly and couldn't travel east, and Anne, never married, didn't want a wedding in Vancouver when home was in the East. So the solution was to elope.

Anne and I thought maybe a church in a small English village would be nice. We could ask a number of English friends to come for lunch and then announce we were going for a stroll to the church as we were getting married. That didn't work, since we would have had to reside in the hamlet for two weeks prior.

Italy was another option, except we would have to be there for a month prior. The Ritz in Paris was suggested, but France has similar rules.

It then occurred to us to check Bermuda. One-week residency prior to the service. Perfect. Mark Twain, who had frequently vacationed there, once said: "You can go to Heaven if you like. I'm staying in Bermuda." We would have the honeymoon before getting married. The date was set: April 11, 1998.

The one thing we didn't think of was that Easter was early that year and a number of Torontonians would be there for the long weekend. So much for the surprise. No one was to know. So who walked into the Coral Beach Tennis Club but none other than Zoe Band (at whose birthday Anne and I first became acquainted), her mother, Sarah, and Zoe's

I Meet the Gem

Anne and I taking our vows in Bermuda. I look as if I've swallowed a pickle.

129

grandmother, Mona Campbell, all there for Easter. I instantly asked Sarah as she entered the lobby, "What are you doing here?"

"The same as you, Foth, to drink rum," she replied.

I corrected her by instantly telling them of our impending nuptials, then asked Zoe to be our flower girl.

We then had dinner with our friends Dick and Beth Currie (Dick being president of Loblaw Companies at the time), who happened to be there for Easter, as well. First we asked if they were doing anything on Saturday morning … golfing or whatever. When it became obvious they had no plans, we asked them to be part of the wedding party. (As Dick later said, it was a competition for best man between himself, the golf pro, and the doorman.) Anne had a girlfriend, Barbara Friedland, fly in from New York City to be maid of honour.

The pleasant spring day turned out to be perfect for a ceremony on the patio overlooking the ocean at the Coral Beach Tennis Club, followed by Dom Perignon and a lovely ride in a calèche into Hamilton for a celebratory lunch at Newstead.

My children and their respectives with Anne and me at our West Coast wedding reception.

I Meet the Gem

We then returned to Toronto to have a wedding party at our club at the Toronto Lawn Tennis Club (where there is no lawn), followed a week later by a wedding party on Bowen Island for the western contingent. And here I thought I was getting off easy with one small ceremony in Bermuda, only to wind up paying for three events. But it didn't matter. It was the best decision of my life.

When we married, Anne had no idea that her vows, "in sickness and in health," would be challenged so soon. Shortly after deciding to get married, Anne suggested that we both get full physicals. After all, it was a new phase of our lives and we should start with a clean slate. That was in November 1997. Numerous tests later with doctors telling me they thought things were fine but one more test just to be sure, I was told the news. I had prostate cancer.

That was three weeks and three days after our marriage, seven months after the initial test, and between our wedding party in Toronto and Bowen Island. A great gift to the bride. We researched the various treatments, which had come a long way in the past ten years, and have fortunately progressed even more since then. In the end, it boiled down to one thing. I didn't want a foreign cancer in my body. The solution: surgery to remove it — a radical prostatectomy.

An appointment was made to see Dr. Michael Robinette in the oncology department at Toronto General Hospital. After discussing the procedure, Dr. Robinette told me I would have to wait another month for the operation, since he was going on holiday. I was shocked (or at least in more shock than I already was). I blurted out, "Whose call is this?"

"Yours," he said.

He cancelled the holiday.

The usual preparations were made. At one point my file was misplaced between hospitals, which resulted in not having enough time to give my own blood for the operation. Around this time Norman Jewison, my film director buddy, called to see how things were going. Anne told him what had happened. He said, "Tell me where to go. I'll give my blood. Better a friend's blood than a stranger's."

I've never forgotten that.

On June 15, 1998, Dr. Robinette performed a three-and-a-half-hour operation to rid me of the cancer. I was lucky. No chemo or radiation afterward. And no recurrence since.

Boy from Nowhere

When I found out I had prostate cancer, I went to my editor Bob Lewis at *Maclean's* and told him. He felt that with my profile it was important to make the public aware of a disease that tended to be kept quiet. Women had been discussing breast cancer since Betty Ford, the former American first lady, openly discussed her illness. But men never discussed anything "below the belt."

PRIME MINISTER · PREMIER MINISTRE

Ottawa, Ontario
K1A 0A2

June 18, 1998

Dear Mr. Fotheringham:

I would like to take the opportunity to offer my best wishes for a full and rapid recovery from your surgery.

I know firsthand the anxiety and uncertainty that accompanies a surgical procedure; not only do you wonder about the outcome but also about the affects on your family and friends. Everyone will surely be relieved, not the least being Anne, when your convalescence is well underway.

While it will be difficult for you to stay off your feet, you should take all the time necessary to regain your strength. My name, for one, could certainly use a rest from your pen.

Please accept my warmest regards.

Sincerely,

Jean Chrétien

Mr. Allan Fotheringham

A letter I received from Prime Minister Jean Chrétien after my prostate cancer surgery.

I Meet the Gem

I agreed, and when I returned to work after a three-month recovery, I wrote an article about my experience. I also became the "poster boy" for the disease for a year, speaking about the disease across the country in the hope that I could help alleviate men's fears and concerns about it.

Through it all I had the strongest woman I've ever met cheering me on. I can't express, even though I make my living as a writer, how much I love her and appreciate her and how I would walk over fiery coals if she asked me. I hope she reads this.

17
On to Hollywood

It all started with an article in a Toronto newspaper written by a retired man who was bored, started going to TV commercial auditions, and signed up with Fulcher Agency, Inc., a talent outfit in Toronto. When Anne saw the article, she suggested I do the same. After all, with my TV experience on *Front Page Challenge* (and, of course, my film debut in *Breakdown* many years ago in Chilliwack), why not? It would be something different, and the worst that could happen was that I would write a column or two about my experiences.

So I went to Fulcher, signed up, and took a mandatory class once a week for eight weeks to learn what I already knew from my television days. I was called for a number of commercial auditions, but nothing came of them. When I read that Fulcher was doing a fundraiser and was putting on a runway show, I thought it would be fun. So for $200 I signed up and forgot about it.

Too much was going on meanwhile. I headed to Saskatoon to receive an honorary degree from the University of Saskatchewan at the same time Queen Elizabeth was there for the province's centennial. I was receiving a Centennial Medal from the Province of Saskatchewan and the Queen's Jubilee Medal. Sandwiched in between was the runway show.

Anne and I had a wonderful week in Saskatchewan. First we went to Saskatoon for the ceremonies and to receive the honorary degree. My son, Kip, brought his two daughters, Quinn and Lauren, to watch their "Oompah" get his degree (Lachlan being too young to come). On arrival at the hotel there was a congratulatory bottle of champagne from our Toronto friends, John and Cheryl Crawford. With Kip and the girls having just arrived, we opened the bottle of champagne for the adults and some Canada Dry (the champagne of ginger ale) for the girls and toasted my good fortune.

Then it was off to the president of the university's home for a celebratory dinner along with the other recipients. Lieutenant Governor Linda

Haverstock was in attendance. Quinn and Lauren were well prepared, having been told they would meet the "queen's representative." When the time arrived, Anne proudly introduced our granddaughters to the lieutenant governor. In awe they immediately curtsied, something they had been practising for weeks. By the end of the evening, Quinn and Lauren had made a friend for life with the lieutenant governor, especially after she sat with the kids on the stairs and presented them with pins commemorating the province's centennial.

I got to know Linda better while on the stage watching the recent graduates obtaining their degrees. She had married far too early, and as a result became a single mom. Determined to get an education, she went back to school and not only got a high school degree but worked hard to obtain a Ph.D. and went on to be the lieutenant governor of her province. A formidable woman.

My address to the graduating students was on the lessons of life. It had been a long day for everyone, and I knew that a speech after getting one's degree was a blur except for the final few words. Mine were: "Don't forget to floss."

Anne and I then headed to Regina for the centennial celebrations. We stayed at Hotel Saskatchewan, a lovely establishment in the provincial capital. Numerous festivities were organized in which we were included, the main one being at Government House where Anne and I attended a special reception for the queen.

At the University of Saskatchewan for my second honorary degree. Chancellor W. Thomas Molloy is to the left of myself and Anne.

Boy from Nowhere

I had met the queen before, both in Vancouver and on the royal yacht *Britannia* in Toronto. But this was a first for Anne. Following the reception, we went to a special royal gala where Saskatchewan's finest talent was featured, including future Consul General to New York (and later Senator) Pamela Wallin and Brent Butt of *Corner Gas* fame.

After that wonderful week in Saskatchewan, we arrived home in Toronto the night before the runway show, which given our busy recent history I hadn't thought about much. To me it was just another fundraiser. I had to be at the York Theatre the next day at 2:30 p.m. for a 7:00 p.m. show with a casual outfit and evening wear. For the grand finale I had a black-and-white outfit (the one I'm wearing on the front jacket of this book).

The organizers wanted to do a trial run, so I went to a large room where the ninety-five male and female participants, ranging from five-year-olds to me, the oldest at seventy-three, were preparing for the big event. I took my newspapers to while away the afternoon but, if truth be known, I learned more about push-up bras and thong underwear than I ever thought I would in a lifetime.

Mothers were putting their darlings through the paces on how to walk down the runway and making sure their makeup and hair were perfect. Numbers were handed out. I was number 321. Why would anyone have a number for a fundraiser? I threw mine into the garbage.

Eventually, the show began. Over five hundred people were in the audience. There were various categories, and I was in the last one called "Lifestyle Models" — a polite way of saying "The Geezer Group."

My first walk down the runway was in a casual outfit. I walked with another man. It all seemed too serious for a fundraiser, so I decided to ham things up. I started "shooting" at the crowd with an imaginary pistol, wiggled my bum at the end of the runway, and headed back to the stage. The crowd went crazy.

Next was evening wear. I strolled down the runway with a woman "of a certain age" in a sequined spaghetti-strap red dress. She was professional and very uptight. When I got to the end of the runway, much to her surprise, I did the Saskatchewan Dip, bending her to the floor, and then turned and wiggled my bum at the audience again. They loved it. My last turn was in the grand finale, and since it was the final act, I curtsied (having just been with the queen, of course). The audience went wild.

On to Hollywood

At this point I went back to the change room to get ready to leave, thinking I had done my part for charity. While collecting my clothes, a large muscle-bound black man wearing a Batman suit and a baseball cap with a grey ponytail came into the room, took my hand, and said, "Come with me."

Rather startled, I said, "I'm not going anywhere with you."

It turned out he was part of the Fulcher Agency staff. He explained I was wanted, since I'd won something.

When I appeared back onstage, the crowd cheered while I received a goodie bag and a plaque. I thought it was the usual giveaways one got at charity events. Only when Anne came backstage did I understand that I'd won "Male Lifestyle Model of the Year" — a $100 gift certificate to one of the finest restaurants in town, a free photo shoot for a portfolio, and $1,000 toward going to the International Model and Talent Association Convention in Los Angeles.

As Anne said, "Dear, you're going to Hollywood!"

I couldn't believe it. Anne, her friend Helene Boughton, and I went to our neighbourhood restaurant, Capocaccia, opened a bottle of champagne, and laughed for hours.

All that happened in May 2005. In January 2006 we were on a plane to California. The convention was at Hotel Bonaventure in downtown Los Angeles where we ran into the vivacious Traute Siebert, the owner of Fulcher, accompanied by Clarissa, her agency director and lovely daughter. Traute told us to enjoy our last few hours of calm as two thousand participants would be arriving within a few hours. And she was right. It was going to be five days of competition and non-stop events.

First I went to the orientation and picked up the kit outlining my schedule. Then I received my number — 6434. This time I didn't throw it in the garbage. First on the agenda was a photo shoot of all the Fulcher Agency participants, which was like herding cats. Finally, they got everyone organized, wearing Fulcher T-shirts and screaming as if we were going to have the time of our lives.

It was the first encounter I'd had with screaming. It didn't stop for five days, whether my fellow team members were on the runway, on the video screen, or performing. Everyone screamed as if The Beatles had just arrived.

Boy from Nowhere

I had to do something every day for a week. First on the schedule was a cold-call read with two hours to practise. I did okay. Next was a one-minute monologue I had to prepare myself. Not one second more, not one second less. If I went over, they would cut me off.

So I said the following:

You know I feel I'm here under false pretenses. I'm a writer, not a speaker. Hence I feel like Elizabeth Taylor's eighth husband. I know what to do, but I'm not sure I can make it interesting. But I've been a journalist for fifty-two years, and young journalists always ask for my advice. Here is what I tell them:

Learn to listen. God gave you one mouth and two ears. Use them in that ratio.

Never argue with a woman. No good has ever come from it.

Travel. It is the best education you will ever get. I have been to ninety-one countries, and that's better than a Ph.D.

Don't get married until you are thirty. If you do, you won't be able to travel, and therefore you won't get an education.

Never play poker with a man named Doc, never order a martini in a town that still has a high school band, and if your mother gives you her age, check it out.

It was exactly a minute. Victory.

Next up was the Real People Competition, which was like a television commercial. So I chose to do one on a car — the Kia Sedona. And dress like a car salesman. I practised for hours and pulled it off. If I ever stopped writing, I now knew I could be a car salesman.

The week sped up. There was no time for anything other than the convention. In between competing, I practised my lines, realizing this was serious business. I was competing against a thousand men, including all the young studs.

On to Hollywood

The convention was the biggest of its kind in the world. And if one wanted to get into show business, this was where to start. Ashton Kutcher of Demi Moore fame, Eva Longoria of *Desperate Housewives* fame, and Katie Holmes of Tom Cruise fame all got their starts here. And now Dr. Foth.

Next came the Talent Showcase, the Sitcom Competition, the (optional) Swimsuit Competition (I took a pass), the Runway Show, the Theatrical Headshot Competition, and on the final day, Callbacks.

I went to Callbacks, and everyone was impressed with my portfolio. One agent said there was work for me in Hollywood, but I would have to move there. (Possibly another career opportunity I had to forgo because another wife of mine wouldn't want to move?) I was also called to do a taped TV commercial, which I did later in the day.

That evening was the Talent and All That Jazz Time when they gave out the awards — a very flashy dress-up affair in which everyone wore stars on their lapels that lit up the room. As with any awards event, it lasted forever. But with this one there were incessant shrieks and screams. After some time, I'd had enough. We left and returned to our room where the phone was ringing. It was Traute. "Where were you? I looked all over for you! You won an award!"

I couldn't believe it. I'd won "third runner-up in the theatrical head-shot division" and the relevant award. (Of course, this being the United States, it was "third runner-up." In Canada it would have been termed "fourth," but no one in the United States is fourth. They are "third runner-up," which illustrates one of the differences between our countries.)

What an experience. Many received scholarships to acting schools, many signed up with agents. Me? I decided to hang up my spurs and return to what I do best. Writing.

18
You Wanna Be a Journalist?

In the mail one day was a polite letter from a young man wanting advice. He was wise because he had come to the right place. Advice is the specialty of this department, offered free on almost any subject under the sun, even on subjects of which I know nothing.

In this case the polite young man wanted some tips on how to become a success in journalism. This is simple, because your humble agent is a world authority on how to become a success in journalism, if not in life. To wit:

Always wear shoes that are smartly shined. It is the first thing a female notices when she meets a man. A wise woman never marries a man who is ill-shod.

Stay away from journalism schools. You can't teach journalism any more than you can teach how to make love. You either got it or you ain't. A matron once asked Louis Armstrong what jazz was. He replied that if she had to ask she'd never know. It's the same as the chap who asked J.P. Morgan what a yacht cost. He was told that if he had to ask he couldn't afford one. Journalism schools fall into the same category.

Never wear button-down shirts with a suit. *Verboten*. Most of American manhood doesn't understand this. It's still *verboten*.

Never accept a present from a politician that can't be consumed at one sitting. The thing to tell the politician is this: if it's a gift, it's too much; if it's a bribe, it's not enough.

You know the definition of an editor. That's a guy who separates the wheat from the chaff. And prints the chaff.

Learn to listen. The greatest shortage in the world is not someone who can explain computers or VCRs, or cheap plumbers or honest lawyers. The greatest shortage in the world is good listeners. Most people, when you're telling them about the leg you broke on the ski hill, aren't really listening. They're just waiting for a break in the conversation so they can tell you about the gallbladder operation they had four years ago.

Most people in the world think they're misunderstood. Especially politicians and high executives. If you simply sit there — interspersing "Gee" or "Golly" or "I didn't know that!" it's absolutely amazing what they will blurt out, all in the belief that at last they've found someone who will listen. That's how bartenders make their money, just mumbling "Uh-huh" while wiping the bar and listening to unhappy husbands. Throw away your tape recorder. Listen.

To quote the immortal Satchel Paige: "Don't look back. Someone might be gaining on you." Never wear cufflinks with a sports jacket. *Verboten.* If a politician asks if he can tell you something off the record, excuse yourself, go to the loo, and don't come back.

The definition of an editorial writer is someone who comes down out of the hills after the battle and shoots the wounded.

Get a good, broad education — while avoiding journalism school — in history, economics, psychology. You don't need English classes, since you're enamoured of literature, anyway.

Travel. It's the best education there is. The reason for travel is not to learn about other countries but to learn about your own. The more you travel the more you'll understand Canada — not an easy country to understand.

Don't get married until you're thirty. If you do, you won't have time to travel and therefore educate yourself. Never join anything. If you do, sooner or later you'll run into the uncomfortable fact that you'll have to write something about one of your new friends — stock fraud, faked expense accounts, groping the waitress, whatever — and you'll lose a friend. The only friend a newspaperman can have is another newspaperman.

Read. If you don't read, you can't write. Be suspicious of everyone. If you watch more than four hours of TV a week, you need serious help. Stay out of the office as much as possible. Newspapers were better before the telephone and the Internet were invented. It meant you actually had to go and meet people.

Take long lunches. You may die of a shotgun wound inflicted by an irate husband, but you'll never die of a heart attack if you take long lunches. Long lunches are good for the heart.

Boy from Nowhere

Be wary of journalists at the Press Club who tell the best stories and can talk very well. Most journalists who can talk very well don't write very well. They leave it at the bar.

Stay away from people you have never seen laugh. They are dangerous, as well as boring. There are more boring people in the world than there are good listeners.

As the wise man said, you have two ears and one mouth. Use them in the same ratio. Pretend that the *I* key on your computer keyboard doesn't exist. Devour five newspapers a day.

19
Death Beckons

My old friend Lord Conrad Black and I go back a long way. Whenever I dropped into London, he would ship his chauffeured limousine out to Heathrow and have me delivered to my hotel.

In the spring of 2007 in Chicago I covered the first two weeks of the spectacular trial that eventually shipped Conrad off to prison. I had to leave because I had a long-standing appointment at a Toronto hospital for a colonoscopy — a routine anti-cancer inspection that my doctor told me had to be done every five years just to be safe. I was told it would require four hours, so I expected to return to Chicago a few days later.

I went in for the colonoscopy on May 14. Afterward, I felt strange. Two days later I collapsed and was rushed by ambulance to St. Michael's Hospital where I was put under observation. A doctor said the hospital would do tests to see what the problem was. Two more days went by without any tests being taken, while my white blood cell count rose.

My wife heard from the doctor, Dr. Ngai, on Friday. He said tests would be done to see why my white cell count was rising. The tests weren't done.

A long weekend arrived, and on Monday the most fantastic thing happened. Somebody, somewhere, pushed the wrong button. The contents of my bowels flowed into my lungs, and I went into septic shock and almost died.

My three children were called in from Vancouver because the doctors said I wouldn't make it. They flew in, thinking the last rites were being read. I was so overly drugged, I didn't even recognize them.

A ventilating tube was put down my throat in an attempt to save me. In the process the doctor permanently destroyed one and a half of my vocal cords. I then got ventilator-activated pneumonia, followed by two hospital superbugs (MRSA and *Pseudomonas*), which colonized in my

Here I am in London, England, reading about Conrad Black.

left lung and which I could only have gotten from the doctors and nurses not washing their hands or the hospital bed that might not have been properly disinfected.

The doctor in charge told my wife that my chances were slim that I would make it through, since so many things had gone wrong. He advised her that she should prepare for the worst, so she sat down and wrote my death notice — not a pleasant thing to do.

To add insult to injury, I then developed pancreatitis. I was in intensive care for six weeks and in hospital for four months. I had a feeding tube for fourteen weeks and went down from 170 pounds in May to 115 pounds in August. I went through a series of seven different drugs to try to eliminate the superbugs. None worked. The eighth one took effect, which was actually the first drug I'd been given, but the doctors had taken me off of it too soon on the first round.

They never thought I'd live, and if I did, I would be permanently compromised. My wife was told to look into nursing homes. She was told I would have a tracheotomy tube down my throat for the rest of my life and quite possibly a feeding tube in my stomach permanently. I was so heavily drugged that for three months I apparently referred to Anne as "Donna," my eldest sister.

I credit Dr. Natalie Wong, who headed up the medical team longer than anyone else, for sticking with my case and eventually finding the right combination of treatments to save my life. And all of this over a four-hour colonoscopy.

In the end, it wasn't doctors or medicine that saved my life. It was my incomparable wife, Anne, who did. Riding shotgun, she came into my hospital room every day through May, June, July, and August. She wore a mask, gloves, and a hospital gown for ten hours a day, made sure no one touched me without washing their hands, had every prescription inspected, and insisted that every doctor-to-doctor communication go through her first. It took her a hundred and forty-five straight days — not missing a single day — to do it. She, and she alone, saved my life.

After Labour Day, I was transported by ambulance to Bridgepoint Health Centre for rehabilitation. I was there for a month before going on an outpatient basis. I was very lucky in that I was given a bed by the window in a "room with a view." My window overlooked the Don Valley

Parkway and spanned from the CN Tower right up the Don Valley. It was September, so I was able to see the leaves turning in all their splendour the whole time I was there. My washroom was directly across the hall, and the nursing station was beside it. Everything was at my fingertips.

Bridgepoint had a wonderful social calendar for patients — movie afternoons, lectures, TV for sports, game rooms. And once each week my wife wheeled me outside to the second-floor deck to listen to live music while we enjoyed ice-cream cones. The food was made in-house, so I actually felt I was getting home-cooked meals. And they tasted like that, as well. I quickly put on some pounds and left at a healthy weight.

Everyone was quite casual in the rehab centre. Having gone through all levels of a hospital, from the ICU on down, being at Bridgepoint was a walk in the park. In fact, there is a glorious park attached to Bridgepoint where I could sit in my wheelchair and see the valley and the city. I received physiotherapy in the mornings and occupational therapy in the afternoons. In between the staff quickly discovered the importance of my getting the morning newspapers. A simple solution to getting well. It was arranged without a fuss.

The staff might be quite casual in the rehab, but that doesn't mean they're casual dealing with patients. I have to think I'm someone who tested their mettle more than most.

When I started feeling more like myself, I decided I wanted to go home for an afternoon, so my wife asked the nurse if she could have my meds before we went out. It wasn't the first time I'd been away, but this was the weekend. The nurse said she couldn't allow me to go out because she didn't have a signed authorization and would have to get in touch with the head nurse, who was off for two days. She then left.

I was determined to see a movie and go home for a few hours, so I got up, dressed, and left. Three hours later the phone rang at our home. The people at Bridgepoint were in a panic. They had searched the entire hospital and grounds. No Dr. Foth to be found. A patient missing? Bring him back at once!

The next day the president of Bridgepoint and various nurses visited me. They told me I was now known as the patient who went AWOL. So I asked the president to take me to rehab. She did and watched how well I was doing. Calm reigned after that.

Death Beckons

It has been about four years since I left Bridgepoint Health Centre. The tracheotomy tube I was supposed to have permanently came out three months after leaving Bridgepoint. No feeding tube in my stomach, either. Do I feel great? I feel terrific — like an eighteen-year-old.

Bridgepoint is in the process of building a new LEED-certified hospital with the intention of being Canada's leader in complex medical care and rehabilitation. It is one of ten in Canada mentioned in an international report stating Bridgepoint is one of the most interesting infrastructure projects in the world. And it is in our own backyard. I, for one, can personally attest to the facility's superior care and attention to its "guests."

I have been asked a hundred times over the years why I didn't sue St. Michael's Hospital for medical incompetence. I discussed it with a number of lawyers and was given advice. But a senior lawyer friend of mine outlined what to expect. When I marched into a courtroom, my lone lawyer would be faced with a virtual army of members of his own profession, not only the hired guns of St. Michael's who were accustomed to years of patient complaints but the lawyer/hacks representing the drug companies, the lawyers representing the insurance companies, and the lawyers representing this and that and who fed me the superbugs. It would take three years to get to court. The stress would be so high that if I was ill, the stress would kill me. If I was well, the judge would say I'd had a bad time but was back to normal now. He would then give me a small settlement, which the lawyers would take for their fees and leave me with the stress. Worth it?

Nice to know this is what they call justice. Life is not fair.

20
My Female Friends

Some time ago Beverley Rockett was the leading model in Toronto — tall, slim, with a vivacious wit. After a long time before the cameras, she bought one herself and became a professional photographer. Moving right along, she became the fashion editor of *City Woman*.

Beverley claimed she had once heard me boast that I knew more about fashion than most women. So she invited me out to lunch in 1983 and tore from my protesting lips these views and also a promise to give her my opinion on the fashion sense of some prominent women, who also happened to be my buddies.

I apparently told her that "fashion intimidates most people. The people I think look best are those who are comfortable with their clothes and do not take them seriously. That's the whole point. My own philosophy is that I dress to amuse myself and to irritate my enemies.

"One of the reasons I'm disliked in the journalistic profession is that I dress rather too well, which makes me suspect. People think I can't be authentic or trusted because I don't go around with a slouch hat or a cigarette hanging off my lip with last week's soup stains on my tie."

Beverley, pressing on, asked me to assess the leading ladies of Canada.

Mila Mulroney

Mila's main asset is her European flair. That was never more evident than at the Progressive Conservative convention. She's like Pierre Trudeau, in a way: it's impossible for her to do anything without looking stylish. She's very European. Yet there's a little-girl quality to her, very infectious.

Maureen McTeer

I remember standing in Ottawa's Lansdowne Park Civic Centre Arena in 1976 when Maureen McTeer and Joe Clark went up to accept the leadership of the Progressive Conservatives. I turned to Marjorie Nichols and said, "Christ, she's wearing one of Maryon Pearson's old dresses." Well, until the advent of Mila Mulroney, Maureen had evolved into the best-dressed woman in Canadian politics. At Joe's defeat by Pierre Trudeau in the 1980 federal election she looked tremendous. She's got great composure and dignity. She's noble, a strong woman.

Barbara Frum

Barbara dressed expensively. She was a good friend of mine, having died too young. She would have killed me if she heard this, but her clothes were a little too busy.

Jeanne Sauvé

As you know, Jeanne was a governor general. She dressed very well in the classic French tradition. French women don't *wonder* if they're dressed well. They *know*. And whatever she did with her hair she did it right.

Sylvia Ostry

Here goes another friendship. Sylvia dresses very expensively, very well, but her accessories are a trifle too busy. A bit too much jewellery. There's understated jewellery and there's overstated.

Barbara Amiel

If I were Barbara Amiel, I would hire myself as my $10,000-a-month fashion consultant. Barbara has the most fantastic body of any seventy-year-old in the Western world, and she doesn't have to emphasize that fact. To conceal is better than to reveal.

Lily Schreyer

Lily Schreyer is a natural who rises to the occasion. Especially with hats. She has a flair for hats. She's not a high-fashion type and doesn't pretend to be, but when she needs to she looks tremendous, which is an extension of her personality.

Anna Porter

My former boss is the best-dressed woman I know who doesn't care about clothes. She's so busy with her career and husband and two kids and grandkids and everything. She has good fashion sense, and if she spent any time, if she wanted to, she could be superb. But she doesn't care and she's well dressed. She's a natural.

Iona Campagnolo

Iona dresses very well but very carefully. The image she projects is of a woman who won't let go. I guess I am trying to destroy my old friendships.

Sondra Gotlieb

Sondra is the most casual of all high-profile Canadian women. She buys expensive clothes, but her personality overcomes it all and you don't really care because you know she doesn't care. She dresses like: "I've only got twenty minutes and I want to see my friends. Let's have a drink."

Chatting with close friend Adrienne Clarkson long before she became governor general.

150

My Female Friends

Adrienne Clarkson

She is the woman I admire the most. I can't recall ever seeing Adrienne when she didn't look dressed for the occasion, whether it was weeding the carrots or whatever. She has the gift of looking as though she doesn't spend a lot of time on how she dresses, even though she does.

In 1994, Beverley Rockett and *Toronto Life* came out with this:

> Allan Fotheringham, columnist and bachelor about town, moved into a new house recently. To mark the occasion, photographer Beverley Rockett decided to give him a gift. Fotheringham adores women — beautiful women, talented women, brainy women, powerful women.
>
> You could almost say they're his hobby. Some men play golf. Others cultivate roses. Fotheringham does lunch with interesting women — including, as it happens, Rockett. So wouldn't it be wonderful, she thought, to make a poster for his new living room from photographs of his favorite lunch dates.
>
> And more wonderful still if they'd pose with him beside the sculpture of young lovers at the corner of Yonge and Shaftesbury. Fotheringham liked the idea and, apparently, so did they, because 21 women turned up on the afternoon of September 7. These are 16 of the photographs Rockett took that day.

"If you want to see the others," the magazine concluded, "you'll have to wangle an invite to Fotheringham's next cocktail party."

21
From a Man I Had Never Met

Written on October 29, 2002, by *Vancouver Sun* Columnist Pete McMartin

Tonight, at a gala dinner at the Bayshore Inn, the Jack Webster Foundation will honour [Allan Fotheringham] with a Lifetime Achievement Award, and it will have been a lifetime ago when I got my first glimpse of him. It was 1976, my rookie year at the *Sun*.

I remember it: he strode up to the *Sun*'s library counter where I had been waiting for some research, and what struck me about him was the unexpected elegance of his clothes — a crisp pinstripe shirt, the cuffs neatly rolled back; a tastefully understated silk tie, loosened at the throat; and knife-creased dress pants, their drape showing the hand of a good tailor. I remember looking at his shoes and feeling stricken, they looked so expensive. He was so groomed he seemed to glint. He struck the fine balance between formality and hipness, which is to say, he was cool. His clothes fit his fame.

This made him an anomaly in the *Sun* newsroom, which was then being flooded by a new generation of reporters like me who saw drabness as proof of our egalitarianism. Our jeans were our uniform. He sought out the Powerful: we sought out the People. He looked like a bon vivant: We looked like hell.

I remember he did not say hello to me as we stood at the counter or, for that matter, notice my existence at all — not uncommon for him, I would find out later. And I sure as hell didn't presume to say hello to him. He was The Man in the newsroom in those days, maybe the last true star the *Vancouver Sun* or any other Canadian newspaper would ever see.

His celebrity was inexplicable to some. He was not the best pure writer the *Sun* had — Paul St. Pierre, Trevor Lautens, and Denny Boyd could all best him on given days.

But he had the ineffable talent of making people want to read him. He was the journalistic equivalent of Julia Roberts — not the prettiest girl in the room but damn if you can take your eyes off her.

My colleague Vaughn Palmer, no slouch of a columnist himself, said of him that he always considered himself first and foremost an entertainer — a philosophy that in the deadly serious heights of High Journalism could rub people the wrong way, and did. That he could back up that entertainment with terrific reporting made him even more intolerable.

His reportage is usually forgotten about him — overshadowed by the smug public caricature and the pundit cracking wise. But reporting was what he did best.

He had a rich eye coupled to a spare economy. Like Orwell — a hero of his — he wrote transparently. Chief Dan George had the face of "a bronzed catcher's mitt." Boxer George Chuvalo had a "cranium of brushed concrete." Of Bobby Orr's spatial genius on the rink, he wrote: "He carried his private piece of ice with him."

He had irony down before anyone else. Writing on a pretentious Vancouver Art Gallery show, he caught all the mutual, silly prejudices of the Generation Gap in one paragraph: "The well-groomed decorous elders who are patrons of the arts come to these openings — so the young can sneer at them. The shiftless wretched dregs of youth come — so the elders can suck their teeth and stare at them. Divided, they stand."

Not that he was all smirk. Spotting a poor lady pensioner buying a powdered meal three days before Christmas — a scene so mundane it would not appear on the radar screens of most reporters — he catches the sadness of a whole world with this passage:

"She invests 41 cents. Pensioners take their boxed, powdered Christmas dinners off the shelves. There's a 1970 trace of Dickens here, lonely flats with gas heaters. The checkout clerk is the real sociologist."

That last line — which comes out of nowhere — is genius. You come away with the whole vignette in your mind despite the fact the sentence doesn't contain one word of description. You can see the woman's careful counting out of change, and the grim pity on the clerk's face; and you can feel the dolour of both their existences. Here is the reporter revealing the world, not just describing it.

That particular came in the youth of his career, when his writing was at its most muscular. Later, when he left Vancouver, something seemed to go out of it, even as his fame rose. The back-page slot in *Maclean's*, the TV gig, the columns tossed off at "38,000 feet over Saskatoon" (meant to impress us, I guess, of his busy bicoastal schedule) — I saw more of his stuff but came away feeling less satisfied. Often his columns seemed too self-regarding, as if he were writing not just about the dealing of the High and Mighty, but his place among them. Hey, everybody! Look at me! It got tiresome.

But then he would leave the daisy-chain environs of Ottawa or Toronto and go somewhere where the world was real, and he would write about it and put you right there. His writing could still transport you.

But it was around this time when I began to hear the first grumblings about his work. He had become too glib. His work had become cartoonish. And worst, the death knell, he had passed his prime. I suppose that is when they give you a Lifetime Achievement Award.

Most of us, of course, don't ever get to have a prime, certainly not me. But his was glorious. When he was at the *Sun* — and that is the part of his career I really care about — he was among the best city columnists in North America, if not the best. His only equals were Pete Hamill and Jimmy Breslin in New York, and there wasn't a soul in Toronto who could touch him. Vancouver didn't know what it had.

I am writing about him today because I think *Sun* readers should know just how good he was, and what the city lost when he left. And I am also writing about him because of an event that, second-hand, brought me into contact with him recently.

It happened after I had written a column about the international Shriners convention that Vancouver hosted this year. Of that convention, I wrote a column which asked the question, "What kind of grown man wears a fez?" The column, which held the Shriners up to a bit of ridicule, attracted hundreds of emails, most of them angry.

Despite the mail — and columnists measure their work by the amount of mail it generates, good or bad — I was unhappy with the column. While I was willing to ask the question about men wearing silly hats, I wasn't willing to answer it. I made my point by implication. I didn't take the column all the way.

But I remembered vaguely that [Fotheringham] had written about the Shriners once, and so I went looking for it to see how he treated them. I found his Shriners column — originally written in June 1971 — reprinted in a slim paperback edition of *Collected & Bound*, a selection of his best pieces from the late 1960s and early 1970s.

These are the last two paragraphs of his column:

> The philanthropy is there, but rather too much is made of it. A hundred years of commerce and horseplay are not yet obviated. There are rather too many brochures, pamphlets and press releases pushed on the extent of good works. If they're done, they're done. Are public relations officers necessary? Do you have to advertise your charity?
>
> It is somewhat like the fraternities which desperately try for publicity for their charity balls to wipe out the memory of the beer busts and the degrees in business management. The wizards and caliphs in baggy pants toot their flutes in the hotel lobby. Beneath those tarbooshes and fake beards lurks a guilt complex.

Can a layman appreciate how brilliant that is, and how much strength of will is needed to see it through? This is column writing at its bravest. It is beautifully written ("wizards and caliphs in baggy pants toot their flutes"), but it is also lean and savage and true. This is what I really think, the columnist says, not what you think I should think.

I read it and felt the pang of envy. My column was pale in comparison. I read his column and I was at the library counter again, looking down at a pair of impossibly expensive shoes, and yearning, secretly, that I might one day fill them.

Didn't happen, of course — couldn't happen. He broke the mould, or the newspaper business broke it in his wake. Maybe all those jeans-clad reporters had their effect. Maybe newspapers became more egalitarian and less accommodating of outsized egos. Maybe nobody came along who could write as well. That era — he took it with him.

Boy from Nowhere

This belated hello, then, from one who you have never met and who should have introduced himself twenty-six years ago when he had the chance.

Mr. Fotheringham, the pleasure's mine.

Courtesy of the *Vancouver Sun*

22
My Greatest Accomplishment

If I were ever asked how I would describe myself, I would say I am a gregarious loner. I enjoy the company of people (particularly women), but as every writer knows, one can only write alone. There was recently a court case, Heather Robertson vs. Thomson Canada Ltd., involving copyright issues with regard to electronic copyright. It was a class action whereby the authors had to put in a list of their writings since 1975. When the administrators saw my list (or more accurately, lists), they said it was mind-boggling. No one had entered a list anywhere close to it. Needless to say, I received the maximum allowed under the ruling. It also indicates how much time I've spent alone.

However, the most important time is not when I'm alone but with my children. As any parent will say about their kids, they are my greatest achievement. Here is why.

Brady Fotheringham

A major gene in the Irish blood deals with stubbornness. As previously mentioned, I was named after my great-grandfather, James Allan, who was born in Ballymena, Northern Ireland (birthplace of the Eaton family.) In 1845 at age seventeen, an orphan, he became a stowaway on a freighter crossing the Atlantic and arrived in Canada penniless and homeless.

My number one son, Brady, has inherited that same bloodstream. After graduating from the University of British Columbia, he set out to emulate his father: journalism and travelling. He wrote a column for a small Vancouver paper and headed out to conquer the world. His father did it by expense account, but Brady had a different weapon: the mountain bike. Never mind that at age thirteen he had collapsed in our garage while playing with brother Kip. He was diagnosed as an epileptic and simply carried on, twenty pills a day, for the rest of his life.

Boy from Nowhere

One day, wandering through Morocco in the Atlas Mountains of North Africa all alone on his bike, he ran into another biker, Tony Shenton, a teacher from England. They got along so well, Shenton shared with Brady his audacious dream — to retrace by bicycle history's most famous trade route, Marco Polo's Silk Road from China. Polo took noodles home, and the Italians have ever since claimed they invented pasta.

Genghis Khan used the Silk Road as he marched from the steppes of Asia, and Polo in the thirteenth century brought back spices and silk from China where an alchemist, Pi Sheng, invented a machine with movable type made of clay four hundred years before Gutenberg.

Shenton checked out thirteen experienced mountain bikers he had met around the world and selected as his mates another Brit, Tim Edwards, and Brady for this 1997 daring adventure. Shenton was fifty-seven, Edwards forty-seven, and Brady just thirty-three. The age difference would later prove, as might be imagined, to be a problem. Brady very smartly had planned at the end of every arduous day to record the day's event in his notebooks and on his tape recorder, with the goal of writing a book if they survived the whole dream.

Marco Polo, who was born in Venice, feasted with Mongol emperors and escorted princesses, leaving descriptive records of his tales. He brought back news of a place called Cathay (China), a land where census takers kept scrupulous records and where cities were connected by intricate canals.

Years after his travels to China, while fighting as a captain on a galley for the Venetians, Polo was arrested as a prisoner of war. Lying in prison in leg irons, he dictated his tales to a romance writer, Rustichello of Pisa, in the cell next door. The writer first published the fascinating tales in French. The world, seen by many as a cloistered fiefdom of the noble rich, soon began to unravel.

What must be the most famous travel narrative in history was now bound in two volumes and was later translated into English as *The Travels of Marco Polo*. Although many couldn't believe the stories of the cultures and foreign land that Polo recounted in his book, Christopher Columbus thoroughly scrutinized his own copy before venturing off to Asia almost two hundred years later. Poor Christopher, thinking he was headed to Asia, sailed the wrong way, ending up in the West Indies. The rest is history.

My Greatest Accomplishment

Brady, with the usual bravado of youth, set out from Beijing with malaria pills, altitude sickness medication, water purification filters, first-aid kits, a small tent, a sleeping bag, a stove with a fuel canister, a half-dozen water bottles, bike tools, thirty-six rolls of film, two cameras, a tape recorder, a few books, gear cables, a bicycle computer complete with altimeter, and fifteen hundred pills (twenty per day for his medical regime). His luggage load totalled one hundred and twenty-five pounds — insane, of course, and a lot of it disappeared quickly.

Ahead of the three bikers was the world's highest pass at sixteen thousand feet where the peaks of the Karakoram in Pakistan put the Canadian Rockies to shame. This was "The Roof of the World" where the four greatest mountain ranges on the globe converged — the Himalaya, Pamir, Karakoram, and Hindu Kush.

Tim Edwards couldn't stand Brady's constant taped broadcasts of his favourite female crooners. Both Tim and Tony had troubles, naturally, with the younger chap's energy level. After three weeks, the Brits found an airport and flew home to London. Brady was left alone, with Pakistan, Afghanistan, and India still ahead of him. He was arrested several times, his heavy load of pills suspected as being cocaine or worse.

He became used to sleeping in ditches beside the road, a rope tied to his ankle and connected to his bike that carried the precious pills that kept him alive. He visited with Pakistani royalty and dined with tank commanders in Afghanistan. Three months, and more than eight thousand miles after leaving Beijing, he arrived in the carbon monoxide capital of New Delhi where he discovered a day there was like smoking twenty packs of cigarettes.

Brady returned to Vancouver to begin his long-planned book. Entitled *On the Trail of Marco Polo: Along the Silk Road by Bicycle*, it was published in 2000 and was chosen "A *Globe and Mail* Notable Book of 2000." The reviews were good, but too many of them insisted on comparing his gifts with those of his father. "Not quite as witty as Dad," and so on. Discouraging, if not humiliating, to someone who put his life on the line to complete such an adventure.

He never once mentioned the unfair comparison to me, but he was clearly wounded by it. And, after what must have been a long period of thought, he announced he was returning to the Orient that he loved where he would be judged on who he was rather than who his father was.

Boy from Nowhere

He is now completing his eighth year of teaching in Seoul, South Korea. His school in the capital is in the richest section of the city, where parents attempt to ship their children to Harvard or Yale, the richest colleges in the Ivy League, or Stanford in California.

Brady doubles his salary, along with the books he writes for his pupils, by writing the application letters to the three U.S. universities — not in Korean English but in American English. He flies to Vancouver for family reunions.

Marco Polo, whose Silk Road journals were without question the original adventure books of the modern world, said it best on his death-bed: "I didn't tell half of what I saw, because no one would have believed me." That's Brady, too.

Kip Fotheringham

There is, as it happens, a young man who lives in Vancouver. He is a senior partner in a lumber-trading firm. He picks up the phone early in the morning and phones somebody he's never met and buys some lumber. He picks up the phone to somebody in Alabama he's never met and sells them lumber, too. It is, I take it, like selling hog belly futures on the Chicago Stock Exchange. Whatever.

He's blissfully happy, with the instant charm of someone being born, as he was, on Valentine's Day. He has a stunningly-beautiful wife, who looks like Grace Kelly and is very quiet. Still waters run deep. An effortless skater, he is captain of a hockey team in a men's beer league and stupidly won't wear a helmet.

In September 2000 this young man — he was thirty-five — went to Houston on business. He encountered some people from an aggressive outfit that was the talk of that Texas town, now the fourth-largest city in the Excited States of America. The outfit was heavy into oil and gas, but didn't know much about timber — while having some pulp-and-paper doings in Quebec. They wanted someone who really knew logs, which British Columbia was built on. They offered him a job, waving tons of greenbacks.

They explained they were such a great employer that they had a hair-dressing salon in their fifty-storey skyscraper so their executives (he being a future one) didn't have to waste time going outside to a barber. They had a restaurant, so their high-flyers wouldn't waste time going out to lunch.

They had in-house doctors and nurses, so you wouldn't have to go outside the building to waste time while you were making money.

They were so powerful, they explained, that they were close friends with the governor of Texas who, while he owned the Texas Rangers baseball team, named the new stadium after the firm. They were so powerful that, great capitalists that they were, after donating $51,000 to Tony Blair's Labour Party, the firm's chairman in Europe was made a Commander of the British Empire. The young man turned them down.

It was now Christmas week 2000. The young man with his brother and sister and his father and the rest repaired, as they did each Christmas, to Whistler to ski. The week was ruined. The Houston boys came back with another urgent offer: a $750,000 U.S. signing bonus, promises of tons of company stock, demanding an answer by New Year's Eve. The young man contemplated his blissful life, one young daughter with another on the way — the wonderful cottage of his in-laws on the Gulf Islands; there was no Whistler in Houston — against the guaranteed riches.

Father drew up one of those yes/no charts: quality of life versus endless money. He agonized for three days over it — skiing abandoned. The Houston boys by now had larded political contributions to 248 members of Congress — two-thirds of all present. They had a lobbyists' office in Washington comprising a hundred bodies. They had given some $575,000 to George W. Bush's political races — $1.9 million to the national political parties, $1.5 million of which went to the Republicans.

Before father could deliver his yes/no chart, son and wife emerged from the bedroom one morning, their decision made. Quality of life beat riches. The Houston boys, of course, were called Enron, an American energy company. A few months later Enron was involved in the largest bankruptcy reorganization in American history up to that date.

The young man, of course, is my son, Kip. We now have a nickname for him — "Lucky." I think the better name is "Smart."

Number two son has always been lucky, when you think of it. Born with good luck, with charm dripping off his elbow. The luck to meet and mate the lovely Jennifer, who can calm and disarm any temper tantrum with a silent gaze that would penetrate platinum. And gifted in the end with three wonderful children who combine their mother's beauty with their father's toss-away sense of humour.

Boy from Nowhere

After Kip graduated from the University of British Columbia, he seemed rather casual for a while in picking out his life's path, actually dabbling for a stretch driving a taxi and doing some bartending. At one stage he considered law school. A little encouraged, I asked my eminent legal beagle friend Julian Porter, who was consistently keeping me out of jail because of libel suits, to have a quiet chat with Kip about the prospects.

Julian took Kip out to the beach one day and walked for an hour with him to get to know him better. Julian's report card: "You don't have to worry about Kip, Foth. He would never make a good lawyer. But what a salesman!" The charm was apparent to the older man.

Mr. Porter's conclusion was correct. Kip is now vice-president of Welco Lumber, the fourth-biggest log exporter in British Columbia, where he has been for eighteen years. His job is simple. Every year he travels to the Orient, from South Korea to Japan and everything south. He travels to Europe, taking in Russia, dripping charm all the way. He does an annual tour of all the major cities south of our border. He knows more about logs than Paul Bunyan.

Left to right: best man Brady, myself, and Kip at Kip's wedding. Boy, we clean up well!

My Greatest Accomplishment

And then there are the kids. Aside from the literary achievements previously mentioned, Quinn plays defence on her soccer team at school. Lauren loves playing women's ice hockey, and Lachlan, who is eight, when not playing badminton, golden locks flying, is going to break a thousand hearts before he is finished.

A movie couldn't be made of a happier family.

Francesca (Fotheringham) Juhasz

Sometimes

Sometimes, we sit quietly
without a word
or gossip for hours

Sometimes, we laugh
or weep
or hug
Sometimes, we reminisce
about younger days

or share poetry

Sometimes, we don't
realize the love
a daughter and father
share

My beautiful daughter, Francesca, doesn't realize it, but she became a *symbol* of the troubles afflicting this strange, underpopulated bilingual nation.

When she began approaching school age, the separatist stirrings in Quebec were just hitting the headlines — headed for who knew where. I wanted her to grow up in a land that respected the two official languages and have her become an adult at ease in either culture. So I put her in grade one at L'École Bilingue in Vancouver.

She continued at L'École Bilingue until grade seven. For grades eight and nine she attended Winston Churchill, a French-immersion high school. For grades ten, eleven, and twelve she attended Magee Secondary, an English high school. And emerged, in far-off British Columbia, as fluently bilingual, at ease whether guiding her unilingual father in trips to Paris, or writing such poetry as displayed above and published in *Vancouver Life*.

Such was her mastering of the language that for several years she was hired to give workshops in other school districts in British Columbia to other grade five, six, and seven teachers teaching in Core French. Along the way she found time to acquire a bachelor of arts from the University of British Columbia, a bachelor of education from UBC, and a master's degree in educational leadership from San Diego State University in California. Her athletic gifts made her a ski instructor at Whistler. Her good looks led to modelling at the Esprit clothing company.

Francesca has been teaching for seventeen years at R.M. Grauer Elementary in the Vancouver suburb of Richmond. During that time, she has taught a variety of grade levels from two to seven. At forty-two she currently teaches a combined grade two/three class in a job-share arrangement, working Monday to Wednesday. She has been married to handsome Bill Juhasz for sixteen years. Bill is currently a principal at Talmey Elementary in Richmond.

Francesca and Bill have two lively sons. Hunter is eleven years old and is in grade six. Angus is eight years old and is in grade three. Both boys attend a French-immersion school in Vancouver called École Jules Quesnel. (Take that, Quebec!)

The two boys play hockey in the Vancouver Thunderbirds Minor Hockey Association, and father Bill has been their coach or assistant coach since they began playing the game. Hunter also loves reading, enjoys caring for animals, plays the cello and also rugby with the Vancouver Meralomas, and is a whiz at rep hockey. Angus is an avid skateboarder and loves practising skateboard tricks at the skateboard park.

A wonderful Canadian family that by its actions reaches out across the land to another province.

My Greatest Accomplishment

* * *

I'm so proud of my children, I could spit.

23
And Then There's %$#&*!!

Every mature nation on the globe has one basic rule: the capital city must be the largest city in the realm. Thus, we have London, Paris, Rome, Madrid, Berlin. All the politicians therein must encounter, in their daily duties, the ordinary citizens who elected them and therefore must learn what all of them have to endure in getting through an actual day.

Immature nations — United States and Canada — ignored this rule and have suffered ever since. In the Excited States of America, Washington, D.C., a small city, is out of the way from average American life. By actual count, there are five lobbyists in the capital for every single member of Congress.

Ottawa, an even smaller city, is a backwater and is populated only by three types — the politicians, the press, and the swivel servants. The only real, live Canadian citizens they ever encounter, day upon day, are bartenders and taxi drivers.

Because the town is so small, all the players know one another. One idle Sunday in 1989, Jean Chrétien found me standing at a hotel news-stand and, correctly assessing that I wasn't doing much, kindly invited me to his house and the family Sunday dinner. We had a lovely evening with his gracious wife, with all the usual lies and gossip.

A decade passed. I was writing my fifth book for Key Porter just as Jean Chrétien was passing the halfway spot in his ten-year reign as prime minister. Publisher Anna Porter had high hopes for the new book and had scheduled an awesome coast-to-coast publicity tour for its pub-lication, from Halifax to Victoria, with book-signing sessions at each stop and interviews with the leading journalists on TV and radio in all the major cities.

The book, entitled *Last Page First*, roams over prime ministers I have known personally, from Pierre Trudeau and Joe Clark to John Turner and Brian Mulroney. In it I have fun with Chrétien, described as the only politician in Canada who can't speak either of the two official languages. Also included was Dalton Camp's celebrated description of Chrétien: "He always looks like the driver of the getaway car."

And I added: "I guess I must have been hard on him in a few columns after that dinner. At the Parliamentary Press Gallery banquet a few years later, those who were not active members of the gallery — I was working in Washington — sat in a separate room. Chrétien wandered in to natter a bit with Charlie Lynch and Bruce Phillips and a few others he knew. He looked down, saw me, and said, "And here's Mr. Fuckingham.""

I finished the manuscript, shipped it off to Key Porter, and prepared for the arduous tour. A month later, after the publisher had stocked every bookstore in Canada with my genius, I got my copy and, filled with the pride only an author knows, started as usual to check for typos.

I got to page 130 and almost fainted. There was the sentence: "He looked down, saw me, and said, 'And here's Mr. Fotheringham.'"

Who would do that? Some minor clerk, perhaps female, who was freaked out at the F-word? Someone higher in the pecking order, who would have Chrétien say something he didn't say and therefore change history? I was blown away, shattered.

Immediately after that I was sent out on the tour that I now dreaded. At every book-signing session I had to turn to page 130 and for every buyer cross out "Fotheringham" and change it to "Fuckingham." At every press interview I had to explain the reason for the change. I was in Winnipeg halfway through the debilitating trip when an agitated Anna Porter reached me by phone. "Foth," she pleaded, "lay off the Fuckingham story. It's hurting Key Porter."

"Are you kidding?" I replied. "Fuckingham is outselling Fotheringham. Fuckingham is gonna make me rich!"

Victoria finished, I fled, exhausted, to my Toronto retreat. All Ottawa, which lives on gossip, was aflame with the mystery of who thought it was okay to censor my book. The phone rang. It was the prime minister. He was on holiday at his daughter's home in Vero Beach, Florida, and said he wanted to tell me a story.

The story was that a week before that encounter at the Parliamentary Press Gallery bash he had been campaigning in Newfoundland and had stopped to have a beer with a group of young Liberal lads. He told them he was having trouble with a columnist who had a difficult last name he couldn't pronounce and could only get as far as "Fodderingham."

At this stage, the PM explained over the phone, one of the lads said, "Why not call him Mr. Fuckingham?"

At last! Proof incarnate that whenever a top Ottawa politician gets into trouble, he has a solution. Blame the Newfs!

My peculiar relationship with Chrétien continued. Anne and I flew to Ottawa where I was scheduled to give a speech at a medical convention. As we entered the hotel room, the phone was ringing. It was the Prime Minister's Office requesting my presence immediately. Once there, Chrétien stated that he wanted to appoint me to a special advisory committee connected to the PMO. I suspected that his staff had checked my age — I was sixty-seven then, two years past official retirement time. Chrétien said, "You mean you're still working?" I told him I couldn't accept any such appointment since with or without a column I still had to be free to carve up his party via TV or radio or books.

Yes. So I'm now approaching eighty and I'm still carving up those who deserve it.

24
The Bohemian Grove

One night, in 1872, five bored reporters at the old *San Francisco Examiner* gathered in a garage loft to promote good fellowship (i.e., booze-ups) and, according to their credo, "to help elevate journalism to that place in the popular estimation to which it is entitled." Good luck. They were the "Bohemian Club" and attracted rather too much attention.

First, the membership was extended to showbiz people, followed by businessmen and, by 1878, the year of the first "Grovefest" out in the woods, the journalists were already on their way out.

Since then "the greatest men's party on earth," according to U.S. President Herbert Hoover, has been accused of everything from kidnapping, rape, ritual murder, Druid ceremonies, and the sacrifice of children. "What night," your scribbler inquired on arriving, "do we eat the babies?"

The Bohemian Grove, in the magnificent Redwood Forest an hour north of San Francisco, is indeed the world's most prestigious summer camp, laid out over two weeks in July. Spread over more than 1,000 hectares to accommodate its 2,200 members, it has 129 "camps" along two and half miles of the ironically called Russian River. (So titled a couple of centuries ago when Russians, crossing from Siberia, came that far south to trap for pelts.)

In truth, it's a wonderful example of why men have stag parties and women have baby showers. These 2,200 guys gather to celebrate what they call "the spirit of Bohemia," says Peter Phillips, a Sonoma State University sociology professor who wrote his doctoral dissertation on the Bohemian Club. "This is a place men can go and hang out with people who are similar to them." Academics who need doctorships will study anything. Wonder what he said about the Rotary Club?

Past membership lists featured William F. Buckley, Jr., Merv Griffin, Edward Teller, Art Linkletter, Ronald Reagan, Gerald Ford, and Caspar Weinberger. The 1971 yearbook shows someone sitting cross-legged on the floor identified as "Lester (Mike) Pearson." Every single Republican president since Hoover has been a member.

Even more impressive than the guest list, perhaps, is the Redwood Forest soaring skyward. There is a stump displayed, perhaps six feet across, that shows its history by the rings growing out from its core.

In 800, Charlemagne was crowned emperor. In 853 the first book was printed in China. The ring marking 953: the text of the Koran finalized. At 1300: Aztec civilization in Mexico. The growth ring signalling 1595: Shakespeare completed *Romeo and Juliet*.

And so it goes, a piece of redwood stump providing a fascinating history lesson, from Leif Ericson landing in North America in 1000 to Joan of Arc burned at the stake in 1431 to Leonardo da Vinci completing *Mona Lisa* in 1506 to Mozart born in 1756 to gold discovered in California in 1848 to Hitler invading Poland in 1939 to the end of the Second World War in 1945. Strange what you can learn from a tree. The oldest tree in this forest is 1,400 years old. It is almost 300 feet high.

The corporate jets at the Santa Rosa airport were lined up impressively as I dropped into Bohemian Grove a decade ago. The food was tremendous, the wine never-ending, the conversation the same.

The music, the most surprising aspect was day- (and sometimes night-) long. And all live. No radios allowed. No TVs. No computers. No cellphones. No crackberries. No taped music and no taping of music. Nothing allowed in but live music. Jazz quartets, classical pianists, symphony orchestras manned by types who gave up the saxophone at university to become millionaires instead. (The reason why this was the most private camp on the globe was, of course, that journalists were banned. Your scribbler smuggled himself in disguised as a chiropractor.)

My old Vancouver friend Jake Kerr sponsored my visit to this magnificent place. He was a long-standing member, as was his father. When he asked me to join him for a week as his guest in July 2002, I had no idea what I was in for.

Jake belonged to the camp called "Land of Happiness." I have a photo of all thirty-four lads sitting on one of the many oriental rugs on the floor of this rustic wooden so-called cabin. In the background is the baby grand piano. Every camp had its own with a guest (or member) pianist. Oh, and their own chef. Not bad for slumming it.

The Bohemian Grove

The "captain" of our camp was Thomas C. Reed, former secretary of the air force during the Reagan administration. We became good friends, and when he wrote his bestselling book *At the Abyss: An Insider's History of the Cold War*, Anne and I gave him a book launch in Toronto, arranged for him to speak at the Empire Club, and secured a television interview with Amanda Lang on her popular CBC show.

In gratitude Tom and his wife, Kate, invited Anne and me down to their home in the Alexander Valley in California, not far from the Bohemian Grove. We had a wonderful weekend and went to the Grove with our wives for the one day of the year that women were allowed in. It gave Anne a chance to see why when I initially called her from the club and told her that next to our wedding day I was having the best time of my life.

Most dazzling were the speakers. At noon every day there was an organ concert followed by a distinguished orator standing beside a 540-foot-long lake covered with water lilies, an obvious imitation of Monet's famous pond at Giverny northwest of Paris.

One day there was a brilliant American academic who explained Washington's idiotic attitude to Cuba. Another day featured a Broadway producer who proved, in an entertaining fashion, the surprising link between Shakespeare and Broadway musicals. Someone else, on another stage, talked about "The Music and Poetry of the Harlem Renaissance." Imagine more than two thousand grown men lying in the grass in their shorts in the sunshine around Monet's little lake.

One morning there appeared at breakfast George Bush, Sr., and Henry Kissinger — my dinner companion at the Canadian embassy in Washington during the Allan Gotlieb days. Kissinger, ever the ham, had performed the previous evening in a walk-on part in a long skit called "Blazing Loincloths," which involved Russians poised to go to war in 1814 with the local Natives over beaver trapping. The table included David Rockefeller, former U.S. Secretary of State George Shultz, and then-present Secretary of Commerce Don Evans, a Texan who was George W. Bush's best friend and who I had previously met at the home of Don Johnson (head of the Organisation for Economic Co-operation and Development at the time) in Paris. Brian Mulroney, at the last minute, had to cancel, I was told.

Kissinger, as ever, went on forever, displaying his wisdom concerning affairs going back to a 1648 diplomatic treaty, not disconcerted at all by the lead singer who playfully ran fingers through the speaker's aging locks.

The senior Bush was the most surprising of all, looking fit and tanned and ten years younger than when he was president — and very witty and sardonic, explaining why he couldn't interfere with his son. None of which your scribbler can report here, of course, because I'm a chiropractor.

In all, it was a most gratifying experience. If 2,200 of the richest and most powerful men in the most powerful empire since Rome wanted to pee up against trees while in their pajamas, at least they did it in style. I'm voting for it. To his surprise, your scribbler thought the Bohemian Grove was a great joint.

While there I gave a speech at the camp on the state of the nation (Canada, that is — most of those in attendance didn't know a bit about my foreign country) and my thoughts on where the new century was going. I felt proud to give a speech in a place where so many intelligent men had spoken in the past. Move over, Henry Kissinger.

When I returned to Canada and wrote a column about Bohemian Grove, all hell broke loose. Everything was supposed to be private and nothing was to be made public once one left. One of the members, Vancouver businessman Andrew Saxton who was an old enemy, read my column and reported it to the club. (Really, Andrew, didn't you think that tattle-tale behaviour was so high school?)

The board almost kicked out my friend Jake Kerr for bringing me. Tom Reed almost resigned. But one thing was certain: I was never invited back. Still, it was one of the best times of my life.

25
Watershed

Everyone gets to the point of having a watershed year. Mine was 2003. In that year Richard Addis, the editor of the *Globe and Mail*, decided it was time to go back to England where his children were living, and in the process pursue another direction in his career.

That direction altered my life, as well. The editor who took his place was Eddie Greenspon. Like every new editor, he wanted to eliminate anything that reminded him of his predecessor, and everything in the newspaper, no matter how successful, that reminded him of Richard.

My column was on the third page. A great position — and very much in keeping with a style familiar in British newspapers on Fleet Street. Richard had decided to have a new photo done of me while wearing a felt wide-brimmed hat. The readers loved it. The column was positively received and widely read.

One day when I was at a function, Ken Thomson (yes, the owner of the *Globe and Mail*, who I had indirectly worked for decades earlier on Fleet Street) came up to me and said how much he missed my column and how he had always looked forward to it in the mornings. But in the newspaper business, sometimes it doesn't matter what the owner likes or dislikes. My column was something Eddie couldn't stomach. So at the end of my contract I was let go.

Months later I was also given notice that *Maclean's* wouldn't be renewing my contract. I was never directly told by Tony Wilson-Smith, the editor at the time (or known in the trade as Tony Two Names). A letter was sent to my agent. No congratulations on a time well spent, no farewell lunch, no gold watch. *Nyet*. After twenty-seven years. What the hell?

Again it was a situation of those in charge not listening. The usual columns stating my departure were written by Tony Two Names and Peter C. Newman for the magazine. Shortly thereafter, Anne called *Maclean's* to get some trivial information, and it took her an hour to get through. When asked what was wrong, the receptionist said there were so many readers calling in to state they missed my column and wanted it back that it was plugging up the switchboard. The receptionist said it was wild. Sometimes it doesn't matter what the reader wants.

So to give credit where credit is due, Tony Two Names tried to replace me. For a period of time, Paul Wells, a fine writer and journalist, did just that. But Paul's strength, in my opinion, is the longer three-thousand-word, well-researched pieces he's known for, not the thousand-word pieces needed for the back page.

That was one of the reasons Michael de Pencier, partner of Anna Porter in Key Porter, nicknamed me "Northern Dancer." He would say that like the famous horse I was short, always fast, rushing to the finish line, on time, and always a winner. No complaints there.

Paul did the back page and then moved on. Next Tony Two Names tried a new way of finding a columnist. Open it to anyone, like the reality shows, and find the new yet-to-be-known Dr. Foth.

Well, it might work with *Canada's Got Talent*, but it didn't work for the back page. So, in a revamp, *Maclean's* cleverly didn't entirely get rid of the back page but turned the last ten pages, give or take, into the back pages, putting the obituaries on the actual last page. I considered it a compliment. In the end, replaced only by dead people no one had ever heard of.

Some might say I had a great run. I *did* have a great run. It was pointed out to me that most people in my position were given the pink slip closer to fifty-five. I was seventy-one. Not bad. But I wasn't ready to throw in the towel.

I flew to Vancouver and discussed my future with Perry Goldsmith, my agent. Perry suggested I do a syndication of my column. He said he wasn't interested in setting it up for me, nor did he want to administer it, but it was something I should consider.

And I did. Never-quit Anne and I got in touch with papers across the country, and in the end with some guidance from Julie Kirsh at the *Toronto Sun*, who had handled my syndicated column while I worked there, I developed the largest *private* syndication in the country. There were writers who had more papers, but their columns went through newspaper syndication or were set up by a company that did nothing but organize syndicating columns.

Watershed

My column ran in papers from the Atlantic to the Pacific until 2007 when I had that run-in with the medical system. I then decided that was enough. After getting better, it was time for my memoirs.

26
Bowen Island

And so your scribbler has arrived on his island in the Pacific. The Bambi and babies leap across the twisting road in front of the rent-a-beast. The fat ferries, looking like big white bugs, float serenely by. And there has been sighting — big news! — of a killer wolf-dog — having taken over from the myth of the sighting of a cougar.

This has been the locale, twenty-nine summers now, for my annual brain transplant, badly needed. Summer with the Fothlets and the mini-Fothlets, with tennis, makes things so serene you can forget Stephen Harper in his Calgary Stampede costume, making him look somewhat like Kate Smith in drag.

This is Bowen Island, just twenty minutes by ferry from Horseshoe Bay off West Vancouver, the sylvan wilderness closest to any major city in the world. Which is why we call it God's Country. Take that, both Toronto and Calgary, and stuff it.

Where else can you wake in the morning, pull up the blinds, and find staring into the window — some ten feet away — a six-point buck deer, looking as if it would like to come in to share the orange juice?

Or look out the other window, across the Howe Sound waters, some fifty miles to see the peaks of the mountains of Whistler where we hosted the 2010 Winter Olympics.

Where else can businessmen, lawyers, and doctors be able to catch an 8:00 a.m. ferry and be in their offices in downtown Vancouver at 9:00 to meet their secretaries? This is paradise, though there is a rumour that it rains a bit in the winter — a foul rumour.

While flying to Vancouver, I told a young man seated next to Anne, "When the sun shines, Vancouver is the most beautiful city in the world."

He replied, "Yes, Mr. Fotheringham, and what day of the year would that be?"

There are minor traumas, of course. It seems the more sophisticated summer visitors have demanded a real golf course. Which, as we know, is the only sport that allows middle-class, middle-age men to dress up like pimps.

The local lads aren't happy, since it would destroy their long tradition of "bush golf." Never heard of it before, since believing that any "sport" where you can ride in a cart is not a sport, but it seems the locals have been content in taking a golf ball into the tangled bush, whack away, destroy the foliage, and have a good time. Tiger Woods wouldn't understand.

Then there is the cougar. Each summer I have been coming here for the transplant and the tennis, there has been a panicky rumour among the mothers that a cougar has been spotted on this mountainous island of some ten miles.

The RCMP posts warnings on the tennis court board. The local weekly, *The Undercurrent*, issues stern warning to families: "If a cougar attacks, pick up your children" and "If a cougar attacks you, fight back."

Since this annual sighting has spotted a single cougar, I have a theory. There is, in fact, one cougar on Bowen Island. He is now seventy-three years old and is having a splendid time, eating Bambi and frightening the locals.

The cougar now has competition: a wolf-dog that's killing dogs, cats, geese, chickens, sheep, and deer. One doesn't wait for an attack to pick up the children — one doesn't let the children out at all.

Alas, the competition is short-lived. The wolf-dog is brought down by a professional trapper. Again the cougar reigns.

There is the world's best newspaper, the *New York Times*, available at 8:00 a.m. at the village grocery store run by a Korean family. The paper's availability is a splendid achievement if you wish to drive fifteen minutes each morning. I don't know how they do it, but it is printed in Oregon, and I guess anything can be done by twenty-minute ferry.

Then there is the African tycoon who arrived from Kenya — he must have known this was the only wilderness island so close to a major city on the globe — and erected an $8 million mansion overlooking the trees. He also built a house for his groundskeeper that is larger than most of the cottages on Bowen. For his daughter's wedding he constructed a special high deck attached to his pad to accommodate the expected six hundred guests, but as they reached a thousand he had to relocate the whole drunk to Vancouver.

And what about the prominent Vancouver lawyer — his father owning much of the local property — who dreamed as a child to build a home on Finisterre, a mountainous rock island some two hundred yards long off Bowen? He erected for his bride an architectural gem overlooking the whole sea, assuming his neighbours would allow him to throw a bridge across the fifty yards of surging tides that separated him from the mainland.

Alas, the lawyer's neighbours thought it would destroy their pristine views. So at dinner parties the man arrives in hip waders and tows his twenty guests across, two at a time, in a rowboat. You might imagine, after the wine, the chaos at midnight.

Perhaps we could return to the cougar.

27
Cast of Characters

Anna Porter

Blond, beautiful, brilliant Anna Porter changed my life.

Just as Peter C. Newman gave me a national audience by putting me on the back page of *Maclean's*, she lifted me from the lowly countryside of journalism up onto the sunny hills of literature. She is a genius.

Anna Porter is a story in herself. Born in Budapest, she was only twelve years of age when the 1956 Hungarian Uprising moved her mother to flee to far-off New Zealand. After she finished her schooling, she took off to London and hooked up with the Macmillan publishing empire that in 1968 shipped her to its Toronto office.

Within a year she moved to venerable McClelland & Stewart, and in time became one of the most powerful people in Canadian publishing. In 1980 she founded her own weapon: Key Porter Books.

One day in Vancouver I received the shortest letter ever written. Two sentences. It read: "Dear Mr. Fotheringham. I think you have a book in you. Next time in Toronto, call me for lunch. Anna Porter."

I obeyed, and when next in Toronto, headed off in a taxi to meet her for lunch. Having read so much about Anna in the national press, I assumed I would find an elderly lady under a shawl but was astonished to see a smashing blonde a decade younger than I. In fact, she was "fifteen months" pregnant, and we had to procure oil to squeeze her out of the banquette once lunch was finished.

What was flattering was that she had divined something in me I'd never thought of. In my sports-writing days graduating into politics, it had never occurred to me to contemplate attempting a book. I realized, talking to Anna, that she had greater ambitions for me than I had for myself!

Being Hungarian, she had three characteristics: a tremendous amount of energy, very strong views about any subject, and a wicked sense of humour. So by 1982 we produced *Malice in Blunderland — Or How the Grits Stole Christmas*, and a year later, *Look, Ma, No Hands: An Affectionate Look at Our Wonderful Tories.*

I then moved to Washington for five years (under Ronnie Reagan and the elder Bush) and under the far-off whip of Anna from afar produced *Capitol Offences: Dr. Foth Meets Uncle Sam* in 1986. The publishing trade as we know is full of the vicious gossip authors distribute about publishers. Anna has two gifts: one is firm, lashing comment about errors or laziness; the other is giant, effusive praise for good work.

And so we continued. In 1989, *Birds of a Feather: The Press and the Politicians*, an explanation of the incestuous relationship between the scribblers and the pols. *Last Page First* came in 1999, and *Fotheringham's Fictionary of Facts & Follies* in 2001. Six books in nineteen years, by which time Anna was my best friend in Canada. So much for author-publisher hatreds.

Anna is married to Julian Porter, who when he graduated from university was the Canadian Football League's first draft choice. He chose law school instead and has defended me in court countless times among

At a picnic in British Columbia. Left to right: my stepfather, Doug Fotheringham; my mother, Edna, seated; sister Donna on the grass; Anna Porter holding her daughter, Catherine; and Donna's husband, Owen, behind.

my twenty-six libel suits. Daughter Catherine, who spoke at my western wedding party on Bowen Island and said she wanted to be me when she grew up, is now a national figure due to her sensitive dispatches from wretched Haiti in her *Toronto Star* columns. Daughter Julia, who works with children with cancer, did all the research for my *Fictionary* book.

Early in 2011, Anna Porter was awarded the $25,000 Shaughnessy Cohen Prize for Political Writing for her latest book, *The Ghosts of Europe*.

Posy (Rosemary) Fennell Boxer Chisholm Feick

Reader's Digest has a section that has been part of the magazine since its inception. It's called "The Most Unforgettable Person I Have Ever Met." In more recent years it is simply called "Unforgettable." My choice is Posy Feick — married three times, each husband richer than the last one.

Posy was one of the last grand dames of Toronto — an era of Chanel suits and fuck-me six-inch heels worn from morning to night. She conducted her life on the world stage and entertained her friends on that same stage.

There was the home in Cuernavaca, Mexico, to complement her penthouse apartment in Manhattan, her palazzo in Venice, and her apartment on the thirty-second floor of the Manulife Centre in Toronto. At one point early on she was a foreign reporter for Toronto's now-defunct *Telegram*.

Stationed in Italy, Posy was friends with the likes of Rudolph Valentino and maharajahs, and spoke of piloting the Aga Khan over the Taj Mahal. When in Rome, one day she received the news of the assassination of Egypt's Anwar Sadat. Immediately, she called Cairo to express her condolences to Mrs. Sadat. Asked how she knew the Sadats, she pondered for a moment and then remembered that Mrs. Sadat had come to one of her parties with King Farouk. That was Posy.

In 2002 I had the occasion to be at a villa she was renting in Acapulco — a change of pace from Cuernavaca. This magnificent villa was built high in the mountains in Las Brisas, a wonderful backdrop for a week not to be believed. Posy had five house guests and people coming and going. Her sister, Nancy, wasn't well, and there were doctors in and out of the sick room most days. Nancy refused an IV and was eventually air-ambulanced to Toronto.

While Posy was dining one night with a Mexican clothing designer named Esteban, probably only famous in Acapulco at the time, his ninety-four-year-old mother drowned in his pool. He returned home to find her there. Posy had a chapel in her villa, so she said she would host the funeral. Meanwhile, friends of hers were staying down the road. When they returned home from a luncheon, they were broadsided by a bus. Posy arranged an air ambulance to get the husband back to the United States.

The phone at the villa rang at all hours while I was there. Posy told friends in India that she would pay for their daughter's wedding. They were on the phone asking for money for the dowry, which Posy negotiated. But the show must go on.

Posy had arranged a party at the villa for the children from the orphanage: piñatas, sombreros, party favour bags, a ten-piece band, hamburgers, and a large cake in the decorated garden. It was a huge success. After the children leave, we were ready to go out to dinner when thirty-five armed military police, administrators, and lawyers stormed the house, headed by the owner.

Apparently, there was confusion over who actually owned the house, and the owner was there to reclaim it. Mayhem broke out. The phone rang as the owner's kids were called and their lawyer was on the phone while faxing legal letters.

Since we were all put under "house arrest," Posy walked out of the bedroom, all five-feet-nothing in hair rollers and a pink silk dressing gown, and put her foot down. No house arrest, she told the invaders. She had paid for a month and she was staying. The owner placed two armed police guards at the door. The rest left.

The next day Posy called Vincente Fox, the president of Mexico and an old friend of her deceased husband. He got hold of the governor who contacted the mayor who called the chief of police of Acapulco. They arranged a special armed unit to replace the two policemen at the front door. Now security was even tighter.

Undeterred, Posy arranged a dinner party at the villa. New guests arrived from Japan with food in plastic containers; they were suspicious of Mexican food. The Japanese saw the armed guards at the door and discovered there was going to be a funeral at the chapel in the house.

They almost fainted. The phone rang again. It was the family in India. They wanted more money for the dowry.

The mayor arrived to check on things and said he would be at the funeral. What more could happen? When Posy left at the end of the month, the owner was there to reclaim his property. And so were the police. They took the owner away; no one has seen him since.

Yet another standard week in the life of Posy Fennell Boxer Chisholm Feick.

Bob Hunter

One Monday morning in 1971, Bob Hunter walked into the *Vancouver Sun* office we shared with Pat Carney, later a Conservative in the Senate, and told us what he'd been up to the night before.

"It was in a church basement," he began, relating how he and a group of equally crazed activists at a meeting had decided to do something about the coming U.S. nuclear test at Amchitka in the Aleutian Islands off Alaska.

Hunter first created a sensation with a book — the first of his thirteen — about his experiences as an uneducated youth working in a Winnipeg slaughterhouse. The blood, the gore, how they slammed the cattle on their foreheads with a sledgehammer before slitting their throats, was something out of Dante.

As he has explained it, Greenpeace was a product of the Vietnam War. Vancouver was sheltering the largest expatriate crowd in the world, "resolutely anti-war to the last love child among them."

This was a generation back when the TV showed every night the body bags coming from Vietnam. While Woodstock still burned, he recalls, "into the public's retina," the last of the Black Panthers were being gunned down, the Eagle had just landed on the moon, some fifty-six thousand nuclear warheads were ready to be fired, a senility case ruled the Kremlin, and Richard Nixon was on speed in the White House.

"If you weren't paranoid," Hunter advised, "you were crazy."

Several hundred of us had gathered in the Citytv studios (only two men in the whole mob wearing ties) to celebrate the thirteenth book — *The* Greenpeace *to Amchitka: An Environmental Odyssey.*

It tells the story that grew out of that Monday morning announcement to Carney and myself. The gunshots that took the lives, Hunter remembered, of Martin Luther King, Jr., and Bobby Kennedy "were still echoing in our ears." Washington had announced it was going to conduct a nuclear test blast off Amchitka Island, Alaska.

Vancouver was the nearest major city to the test zone at Amchitka, even if it was protected by Vancouver Island from any tidal waves that might be triggered by the blast. Hunter and his Greenpeace buddies were going to sabotage the nuclear test.

All in madness, of course, they found an old eighty-foot halibut seiner, the *Phyllis Cormack*, captained by the fearless skipper, John Cormack. Hunter recalled: "I doubted my own sanity and was completely befuddled by the experience of forty-three days on a boat with eleven other crazies."

As it happened — Vancouver going nuts with the daring adventure while Hunter dictated copy to the *Vancouver Sun* news desk every day — the sleepy old fishboat would never get to commit suicide in the nuclear blast zone in time.

Hunter had come up with the idea of starting a committee called Don't Make a Wave, which would sail to Alaska to block the explosion. He told us that, as he walked out of the church basement, he raised his hand aloft in that familiar 1960s hippie sign and said, "Peace."

A young social worker replied, "Make it a green peace."

And so this young man from Winnipeg, the first president of Greenpeace by 1973, led the organization through its transformation into what it is today: an international group present in forty-one countries, with more than 2.5 million members worldwide. *Time* once named Hunter one of the top environmental heroes of the twentieth century. He died in 2005, only sixty-three years old. He also changed the world.

My friend and I were a strange dichotomy. I had worked on Fleet Street in London, in the Ottawa Press Gallery, and in Washington covering the White House; Bob, a decade younger, got his education in that Winnipeg slaughterhouse and as a copy boy at the *Winnipeg Tribune*.

I lived with my practice wife in a plush home in the Kerrisdale neighbourhood of Vancouver; Bob lived with his young family on a houseboat on the Fraser River. Yet we were both left wing and anti-establishment. I liked this bearded, dishevelled hippie — his language, the strange cigarettes he smoked, his contempt for authority. Even his humour, which always ended in a self-mocking, high-pitched giggle.

When we worked at the *Sun*, I had been yearning for years for my own political column. But these were the anti–Vietnam War, pro-pot years, so our managing editor, Bill Galt, decided he needed someone who could explain and relate all of that to our readers.

That was how Hunter — to his great glee — became the first counter-culture columnist in all of Canada's newspapers. I eventually got a slot where I could do my dull political stuff, but meanwhile we became close friends, matching insult with insult.

Hunter and his crewmates didn't succeed in their first quest to stop the nuclear explosion at Amchitka. Their sagging halibut seiner — which became *Greenpeace I* — was blocked by the U.S. Coast Guard from getting near the island, and the underground bomb was eventually detonated. But the *Vancouver Sun* columnist aboard filed a dispatch every day of the epic forty-three-day journey.

Hunter's daily reports made headlines across North America and, eventually, the world. In the process these early activists won the battle. Washington became aware of the power of Greenpeace, which now had a growing international following. Amchitka was never again used as a nuclear site.

However, while the United States, along with Britain and the Soviet Union, had agreed to stop atmospheric tests and to restrict its explosions underground back in 1963, France and China hadn't made such a commitment. France was performing nuclear tests above ground on islands in the South Pacific, and in 1972 Greenpeace eco-warriors decided to try to put a stop to it. But French warships surrounded their vessel, one coming so close that it collided with a Greenpeace vessel, causing so much damage that the organization had to abandon the mission that year.

In 1973 officials boarded a Greenpeace boat and beat the skipper so severely he was partially blinded in one eye. One of the activist crew members photographed the incident and was able to smuggle the film ashore. News of the beating was reported around the globe.

In 1985, when French secret service agents blasted a hole in the side of Greenpeace's the *Rainbow Warrior* as it prepared to sail to a South Pacific nuclear test site, Greenpeace photographer Fernando Pereira was killed. The French government eventually admitted to sanctioning the attack.

The *Rainbow Warrior*'s destruction ultimately helped turn the world against nuclear testing. The birth of Greenpeace and its protests brought public attention to the hunting of whales, as well as to the dumping of toxic waste into the oceans. Inspired by Bob Hunter's style of attracting publicity — Greenpeace activists blocked oil tankers, hung banners on New York's Statue of Liberty, and climbed Toronto's CN Tower — the world woke up.

Hunter ended his journalism career — though he readily confessed that he was a traitor, since his writing was always opinionated — doing a regular breakfast-time gig on Citytv in Toronto. On camera in his dressing gown he'd go through the morning newspapers, explaining to viewers the slant and distortion depending on each newspaper owner's political persuasion.

When he lost his long fight against prostate cancer, his death didn't go unnoticed. It made headlines in North America, Europe, and Asia. Scotland's parliament passed a motion mourning and applauding him.

At his memorial service nine speakers gave their tributes, including two of his children, Conan and Emily, and Bobbi, his wife of thirty-one years. Dalton McGuinty, premier of Ontario, told those gathered that Hunter was "a citizen of the world who had altered history." Prime Minister Paul Martin sent his condolences.

Paul Watson, with whom Hunter faced down a sealing ship on ice floes off Labrador, announced that a new ship dedicated to research and activist campaigns would be named the *Robert Lorne Hunter* and — to unending cheers — that "Bob is going back to sea."

Everyone leaving the service was given a tiny seedling, accompanied by a note:

> Embrace your friends
> Love your family
> Celebrate all life
> And hug this tree
> For me
> Love, Bob

Cast of Characters

My little tree is flourishing, as are my memories of a lifelong friend whose idealism helped change the world.

Ed Schreyer

Socialists, so goes the myth, have no sense of humour. Too idealistic, too starry-eyed in their beliefs.

Tommy Douglas, who introduced medicare to Canada as Saskatchewan's premier, disproved that idea. Campaigning to a group of farmers one day, the five-foot-five midget had to stand on a manure spreader to be seen. He opened his speech: "This is the first time I have ever stood on the Liberal Party platform."

Ed Schreyer, at twenty-two the youngest NDP MLA ever elected in Manitoba, followed in Tommy's path as his province's premier from 1969 to 1977. In 1979 he became the first socialist to be appointed governor general and continued in that office until 1984.

While Ed was governor general, author Farley Mowat, Newfoundland artist and printmaker David Blackwood, humourist Don Harron (also known as Charlie Farquharson), and myself were regulars at both Rideau Hall in Ottawa and the Citadelle in Quebec City, especially on their respective tennis courts. In fact, decades later, because Anne was on the board of the Canadiana Foundation and one of the meetings was at the Citadelle at the invitation of Governor General Michaëlle Jean, I told the governor general that I used to play tennis with Ed Schreyer, Farley Mowat, and the boys. I asked if the tennis court was still there. Madame Jean responded

Greeting Lily and Ed Schreyer at Rideau Hall in Ottawa, along with my companion, Mary Kelly.

in the affirmative and invited me to come back another time for a game. Now that I have a new knee and play regularly, I'm ready to go back to the Citadelle for that match. The only problem is there is a new governor general — David Johnston. Ah, Your Excellency, Mr. Johnston, tennis anyone?

Schreyer's earnest manner disguised a wide-ranging mind. He found the endless medal presentations and museum openings endemic to the job less than, uh, challenging to that mind. Because the constraints of his title removed him from political discourse, he sought out interesting dining companions he could argue with.

I was going through a seventeen-year bachelor spell when Schreyer was governor general, and was a regular diner at Rideau Hall, along with Ed's vivacious wife, Lily, whose laugh was the most delightful thing at the table. One night, two dozen of us were in the dining hall with usual suspects Farley Mowat and Don Harron. And also Alexander Yakovlev.

Born in a small village near the Volga River, Yakovlev fought in the Red Army during the Second World War before becoming a Communist Party apparatchik. By the 1960s, he had earned a senior post in the ideology department of the Central Committee.

Showing off my great tennis style at Club Med in Turks and Caicos.

A reformer from his early days, Yakovlev sought ways to open the Soviet Union to the West and in 1972 helped organize the Canada–Soviet Union Summit Series, despite a skeptical Politburo that feared the Soviet hockey team would be routed. Later that year he went a step too far by publishing an article condemning Russian nationalism and anti-Semitism. He was banished to Canada where he served as Soviet ambassador from 1973 to 1983.

It was in Canada, Yakovlev wrote in his book, *Maelstrom of Memory*, that he began to profoundly question Soviet ideas. "I gave 10 years of my life to Canada," he wrote. "I carefully studied Canadian life. It was a simple, pragmatic life, based on common sense. I wondered why we in the Soviet Union refused to give up our dogmas. My instructions from Moscow — to criticize Canada and to promote our propaganda — seemed silly to me."

He developed a close friendship with Pierre Trudeau, and when the prime minister's second son, Alexandre, was born on December 25, 1973, the family nicknamed him Sacha, the Russian diminutive of Yakovlev's first name.

In 1983, as his decade-long assignment was coming to an end, Yakovlev invited Mikhail Gorbachev, then the Soviet agriculture boss and a rising star in the Kremlin, for a ten-day tour of Canadian cities and farms. During a visit to Minister of Agriculture Eugene Whelan's farm near Windsor, Gorbachev and Yakovlev asked to be alone and took a walk in a nearby wheat field.

"We were alone in the field. Security people, both Canadians and ours, were away on the side, and something just snapped," Yakovlev said in a 2003 interview with the CBC. "He talked about the situation inside our country, about how everything had to change, and so, choking on our words and having completely lost control of ourselves, we agreed that if things continued as they were, it would end up badly. So this was a very serious discussion. Eighty percent of it later became real during the perestroika years."

Yakovlev and Schreyer became close friends, and on the Rideau Hall evening in question, the governor general came up with one of his mischievous ideas. He decided the argument that enlivened dinner should proceed, along with the brandy, to the conservatory for a formal debate.

Mowat, along with your faithful agent, was assigned to defend the joys of capitalism. Yakovlev promised to convert us to communism. Harron was ordered to be moderator. An amused Schreyer sat shotgun, and the other guests reeled back at such formidable brain power.

For several hours the battle raged. Orchids cowered beneath the verbiage, and entire palms bent with the wind power. Memory obliterates the victor.

After Gorbachev became Soviet leader in 1985, he named Yakovlev to a number of key posts and had him draft the first Kremlin policy on perestroika and glasnost. Two years later Yakovlev became a full member of the Politburo and led the battle for political freedom against the orthodox wing of the Communist Party.

He encouraged and protected journalists, writers, artists, and filmmakers who challenged decades of Soviet dogma. He also supported political reforms that ended the party's stranglehold on power and exposed the secrets of the gulag and the mass executions under Joseph Stalin.

Denounced by hard-liners, Yakovlev quit the Communist Party in August 1991 and warned of an impending coup. Three days later the hard-liners launched their botched attempt to seize power. By December the Soviet Union was dead.

The prestigious *Washington Post* traced the birth of perestroika to Ottawa. I wrote a column in the *Globe and Mail* about our momentous Rideau Hall debate. The next morning a letter to the editor appeared in the *Globe*: "If Farley, Harron, and Fotheringham, in fact, brought down the Berlin Wall, we surely know the world is in trouble."

John W. H. Bassett

The likes of John Bassett don't come this way too often. Most people know the name because he owned the now-defunct *Telegram* in Toronto. He started Baton Broadcasting, which ran the TV station CFTO-TV, and eventually took over CTV. At one point he was part owner of Maple Leaf Gardens Limited and became president. But other than playing tennis occasionally with him and attending his famous parties, I knew John Bassett as the man who saved a girl's job at the bank.

Cast of Characters

In the fall of 1997, Anne and I were having a farewell dinner for a very good friend of ours, Gillian Johnson, a former member of the Canadian national speed-skating team and the baby sister of Senator Janis Johnson, a former girlfriend of mine. Both are daughters of the now-deceased Dr. George Johnson of Gimli, Manitoba, who delivered every baby in the environs, thus having the local school named after him. He was health minister in the Duff Roblin Manitoba government and was later appointed lieutenant governor of the province.

Gillian had been staying with us for a couple of months, having left Manitoba to try Toronto on for size. Eventually, she moved to England to marry the writer Nicholas Shakespeare, a cousin thirteen times removed of someone called William Shakespeare.

We suggested Gillian make up the guest list for the evening. One guest was Linda Robinson, a lady friend who was chief actuary to Al Flood, the CEO of the Canadian Imperial Bank of Commerce. This was a Saturday, and Gillian was concerned that Linda was going to be fired on Monday unless she had a good explanation why she was always late for work. It didn't matter that Linda worked most nights until midnight. It was a bank, and everyone was expected to keep banking hours at the very least. Linda, though, was incapable of rising early and being alert in the morning. She was a nighthawk, and the morning was lost on her.

I proceeded to tell Linda a tale that John Bassett had told me at a dinner party in the Bassett home. Early in the Second World War during the fighting in France, John was a major with the Seaforth Highlanders under Colonel Budge Bell-Irving from Vancouver. They were to attack at dawn. John asked his superior why they had to "attack at dawn." Why not in the afternoon? It was explained that the military manual stated that was how it was done. Bassett suggested they have lunch, a snooze, and then go after the enemy.

One would question why John requested the change. A better time to attack? Throw off the enemy? Better the troops be fortified with a good lunch under their belts? No, John hated mornings. So, after lunch and a snooze, they got down to business. The result? At 4:00 p.m. they found two hundred German soldiers in their shorts sunbathing on the grass by the riverbank. Not a bullet was fired and there wasn't one casualty. All the Germans were captured.

Then, for Linda's benefit, I recited Winston Churchill's famous speech to the British on June 4, 1940: "We shall go on to the end. We shall fight in France, we shall fight on the seas and oceans, we shall fight with growing confidence and growing strength in the air, we shall defend our island, whatever the cost may be. *We shall fight on the beaches*, we shall fight on the landing grounds, we shall fight in the fields and in the streets, we shall fight in the hills; we shall never surrender ..." (As you might imagine, it was quite a dinner party.)

When I finished, I told Linda to go in with this ammunition and give her bosses a speech that would blow them out of their boardroom chairs.

Armed with these important historical moments, Linda went into the meeting the following Monday morning and recounted the Major Bassett story, adding the full blast of Churchill's speech. Needless to say, Linda's job was saved by Colonel Bassett and his helper, Winston Churchill.

I wrote John Bassett and told him what had transpired and how he had saved Linda's job at the bank. His letter, dated November 6, 1997, stated that he was thrilled to be of some help in saving her job. All that I had stated about the capture was true, and he also liberated a jeep the Germans had seized from the British at Arnhem. Since company commanders didn't have their own jeeps, this was a great feather in Bassett's cap.

At this point John had been bedridden for quite a while. His wife, Isabel, told me later that my letter so inspired him that he decided to have a party. He was working on the details by himself and wanted no assistance. He was organizing tables and the menu, but as bad luck would have it, his appendix burst and he had to go into the hospital. He never came back.

They just don't make them like John Bassett anymore.

Bobby Kennedy

I never liked Bobby Kennedy from afar, thinking him an arrogant little dink. In 1968 he was going to Oregon for the second-last primary in his late bid for the presidency before the final primary a week later in California. I drove my car down from Vancouver and followed him for a week as he travelled through Oregon. During that trip, I changed my mind about Bobby, now finding him a very sincere and thoughtful person as he pleaded his case throughout rural Oregon.

Cast of Characters

When I returned to the *Vancouver Sun*, I wrote a long op-ed piece about Kennedy, finishing up with a sentence that despite his venture to California he was "dead." Cliff MacKay, the *Sun's* editor, dropped into my office and said, "Allan, I know you mean he's politically dead, but considering what's gone before him in the family, wouldn't you like to change that to being 'politically dead'?"

In my youthful arrogance I insisted, "No." I wanted the sentence to be left the way I'd written it.

A week later my practice wife and I were watching the California Democratic primary vote. It was 11:00 p.m., and she got up and said she was going to bed. I asked, "Aren't you going to wait for the vote result?" As it happened, our friend Norman Jewison was going to have dinner with Bobby the night of the vote.

Sallye said, "No, the Americans are crazy. They killed John Kennedy, they killed Martin Luther King, and they'll kill Bobby Kennedy."

Two hours later I went upstairs and woke her up. She was right.

Bobby Kennedy was a good friend of John Bassett. In fact, John was a pallbearer at Bobby's funeral. When John died, we were in the church waiting for John's service to begin, but there was a delay. It soon became apparent why. Ethel Kennedy arrived (her plane was late), walked to the front of the church, greeted the Bassett family, and sat beside them. The service could now begin. Everything was fine with the world.

Twice after the Bassett funeral I visited my friends Dick and Beth Currie in Jupiter, Florida. On two occasions we dined at a restaurant where Ethel was, as well. Both times I walked over to her to reminisce about good lost friends.

Joe Clark

The most famous of my jaunts with politicians was when I travelled around the world with Joe Clark. The Conservative Party thought that because Joe was so young and inexperienced, he needed some gravitas and should get to know a few foreign leaders. We were to take off in January 1979, so Clark's office sent me the itinerary the previous December. I took one look at it and could see the trip was going to be a disaster.

Boy from Nowhere

The Tories dispatched Joe to Hawaii to rest up for the coming excursion so his mind would be sharp and his body in shape. The press and television people were to meet him in Tokyo, setting off from Vancouver. So, sitting in Hotel Vancouver, we told Joe's press secretary, Donald Doyle, who was from Quebec, that if the trip took place without any disasters, we would buy him free drinks all the way. I don't think the press agent had ever travelled much, either. When we got to Tokyo, we showed some Tokyo-based reporters in the Tokyo Press Club the itinerary. They fell down laughing.

The Japanese reporters' mirth so frightened two Canadian reporters, one of whom was Bob Lewis of *Maclean's*, that they booked direct flights from Tokyo to New Delhi, skipping the scheduled refuelling in the Philippines. I told Lewis, "The number one rule of journalism is 'stick with the story.' If Joe Clark drowns over the South China Sea, you've got to be there to report it." He cancelled his New Delhi ticket and repeats that mantra to me to this day.

The airline Clark's people had booked was Egypt Air, which we later learned had the world's worst accident rate. When we got onboard, there were bullet holes and blood on the headrests. The plane ran out of liquor

Joe Clark speaking to Indian Prime Minister Morarji Desai in 1979 while I listen to Clark's explanation of losing his underwear.

almost immediately, and the press needed it badly. We arrived in the Philippines too late to transfer to the Lufthansa flight to New Delhi. The Germans had waited over an hour for us and were about to take off, so all we could do was race across the tarmac and barely make it before they shut the doors. As a result, when we arrived in India, Joe's people had not only lost all of his underwear but had left behind the TV cameras, tape recorders, and typewriters that were to record this triumphant journey. Joe Clark never recovered from losing his underwear.

We moved on from New Delhi to Jerusalem where on the Golan Heights, inspecting a Canadian brigade holding their weapons aloft in the usual formal salute, Joe walked into a bayonet. I interviewed the soldier involved, a nice kid from Nanaimo, British Columbia, and he told me, "I could see him coming. I knew what he was going to do, but I'm not allowed to move."

Next was Jordan where Joe's quotes became even more famous. At a farm he asked the farmer, "What is the totality of your acreage?" At another farm he asked the owner, "How old are the chickens?"

In Jerusalem, Clark met with Prime Minister Menachem Begin to discuss moving the Canadian embassy from Tel Aviv to Jerusalem. When Begin entered the room, he couldn't figure out who was the prime minister of Canada. "Clark has a small magnetic field," as Dalton Camp once described. At the arranged meeting with opposition leader Shimon Peres, Joe came into the small room, which had about ten chairs around the table. Peres obviously had a Cabinet meeting and was late. Peres then invited the press to stay. Joe stood there stiffly … for an hour. Yet another opportunity for the press to watch Joe's bumbling. You can hate a politician if you like, but once they start laughing at you, you're finished. That trip, because he had such a young and callow staff who couldn't read an airline schedule, finished Joe off, and that's why he lasted only nine months at 24 Sussex.

The first time I met Joe Clark was for coffee in a little café on South Granville in Vancouver. He was from small-town Alberta, High River, and I was from small-town Saskatchewan, Hearne. The first thing that impressed me about him — I being the hotshot columnist with the *Vancouver Sun* — was that his hands shook so much over his coffee cup that he could barely control it. I presumed he knew he was going to get assassinated, as I guess I did.

High River is about fifty miles south of Calgary. It was the home of W.O. Mitchell, whose wife, Merna, was a swimming instructor and tried to give Joe swimming lessons. Years later, when Joe became prime minister, I was ushered into his office on Parliament Hill to do a tape-recorded interview with him.

As usual Joe's press secretary sat behind him with a tape recorder to ensure I wouldn't make things up. I asked Joe about those swimming lessons in High River, and he said they were a disaster because — I broke in and said, "Because your head was too light."

"No," he replied. "It was because my head was too heavy."

The press secretary, who I could see over Clark's shoulder, threw his hands to his face, seeing the disaster ahead. I left the interview and went to the National Press Club for lunch and told everyone to their great glee that Joe Clark had just given me on my tape recorder a statement that his head was so heavy that he couldn't swim. I played them the tape, and every Parliament Hill reporter rushed out with the scoop. The story ended up on the front pages of every paper in Canada the next day, verifying for Canadians that they had elected a goofball. That's why Joe only lasted nine months in office.

When Finance Minister John Crosbie introduced his budget of "small pain for no gain," Bob Rae, then the bright young NDP MP from Toronto, moved a no-confidence motion in December 1979. (If Rae had stuck with the NDP, perhaps he'd be leader of the opposition now.) The morning before the motion was to be voted on, Clark held his usual staff meeting. After they went through routine business, Joe was about to adjourn the meeting and asked if anyone else had anything to say. A shy young twenty-five-year-old, Nancy Jamieson, said, "Yes. You are going to lose the budget vote tonight."

Clark paid no attention to her because she was not only a minor staffer but she was a female. (Later she rose to quite high rank in the CBC.) As it happened, the callow and green Clarkians who couldn't keep track of their underwear on a global tour couldn't count correctly on December 13 and lost the budget vote, a government, a subsequent election, and eventually, their political careers.

My wife, Anne, was first introduced to Joe Clark at a Politics and the Pen soiree in Ottawa. When I encountered Joe and his wife, Maureen McTeer, I said to Joe, "This is my new bride, Anne."

Without a blink, he said to her, "You are a strong woman."

Nelson Mandela

One day I received a phone call from a contact who said he thought I should go to South Africa next week because something important was going to happen. I figured it had something to do with Nelson Mandela, who had been held in prison by the white government for twenty-seven years. I was right. Mandela was about to be released. That was February 11, 1990. Because of the security concerns, no traffic was allowed within five miles of the comfortable lodgings he was then in with white servants. I was with English journalist Christopher Wren, who wrote for the *New York Times* and was a direct descendant of the architect who had built St. Paul's Cathedral in London. Chris and I strode five miles in and five out on that historic day.

Years later, in 2002, Gerry Schwartz, one of the richest men in Canada, and his wife, Heather Reisman, hosted a prestigious evening for Mandela and his wife, Graça Machel. In attendance were Gordon Nixon, president of the Royal Bank of Canada; Leonard Asper, CEO of CanWest; and Buzz Hargrove, president of Canadian Auto Workers. Also invited were numerous high-class people in Toronto and selected others such as actors Michael Douglas and Catherine Zeta-Jones.

The event was a fundraiser for the Nelson Mandela Children's Fund, one of Mandela's charities. Ray Heard, journalist and former communications director to Liberal Prime Minister John Turner, had initiated the idea of making Mandela an honorary citizen of Canada. Heard contacted the Prime Minister's Office, and Jean Chrétien and Finance Minister Paul Martin jumped at the opportunity. Ryerson University also gave Mandela and his wife honorary degrees. All that, along with the fundraiser guaranteed to raise $1 million, led to Mandela's visit.

Boy from Nowhere

Tickets to the fundraiser were $5,000 per couple. The promise was that guests in attendance would get their pictures taken with Mandela. I went over and introduced myself to the man, telling him that I'd been in Cape Town and had seen him released from prison. There must have been two thousand reporters from all over the world who had gathered there for that historic day. Mandela said to me, "Oh, yes, Mr. Fotheringham, I remember you." That's a classy guy.

The Schwartz house had been rigged with heavy TV lights. When the first signature was about to take place, a button was pushed to turn on all of the powerful press lights, which blew out a transformer. End of photo shoot. End of the evening. All the high-priced socialites slunk out quickly to their limos. Gerry Schwartz still hasn't recovered.

Mandela managed to leave the room and go to the bottom of the staircase in the entranceway to give a speech. It so happened that Anne and I had placed ourselves on the first step to get out of the way of the mayhem. So when the Toronto newspaper photographers got a shot of Mandela for the front pages of the next day's editions, in the background was former Prime Minister Joe Clark, Anne, and myself. We are the only ones to have a memorable photo of the evening for all the country to see.

John Laxton

One night I threw a large party at my home. It was attended by all the lads who had graduated from UBC's law school, together with their wives. At one stage in the evening, while the gargle flowed, I noticed the whole gang had backed one of their number up against the wall and were sneering at him.

The man being taunted was a fairly small fellow with a bad English accent. He was being ridiculed because, as a devout socialist, he had made a lot of money. I didn't like the odds and what was happening. So I went over, stood beside him, took his side, and began to destroy some of his tormenters' arguments. The noise attracted all of the wives in the kitchen. They came out and acted like a chorus, taking sides in the argument, cheering one side or the other as the debate raged. At the end they judged that this complete stranger and I were the winners against the mob. So I turned to him, introduced myself, and asked, "Who are you?" He said his name was John Laxton, and we became lifetime friends.

Cast of Characters

John was a poor boy from the north of England. He escaped from there with his bride, smuggling her under darkness of night over the stone wall around her rich high-class family's mansion. They landed in Montreal, hated the snow and ice, and decided to drive to Calgary and get jobs. The day they hit Calgary there was a massive snowstorm, so they kept driving. Arriving in Vancouver on a magnificent sunny day, they were so mesmerized by the mountains and sea that they continued motoring through the city without stopping until they came to a cliff in West Vancouver, got out of the car, and gazed at the ocean.

Today Laxton, very rich, has a house designed by Arthur Erickson, Canada's finest architect. It's on that very spot on that same cliff. John became chairman of BC Hydro, put there by a B.C. socialist government, and owns along with other huge Vancouver projects a terrific home in Baja California, which he loaned to my childe bride and me for a week as a wedding gift. John ruined one marriage due to his mania for running marathons and training for them, and he still works out every day in the gym.

Pierre Berton

A dull professor put out a book about the Swordmen's Club, which was an open secret in literary circles in Toronto in the 1960s and 1970s when Jack McClelland and Pierre Berton had monthly lush lunches featuring young secretaries from their firms. The lunches went on for five hours and ended up in bedrooms upstairs. Ken Whyte, who was editor of *Saturday Night* in the mid-1990s, knew that although I wasn't a Swordmen's participant, I was supposedly on the inside, and offered me $20,000 for an article revealing the scandal (an exorbitant fee for those times). I told him I couldn't possibly comply because Pierre was a friend. The next time I saw Berton I told him rather proudly how I'd turned the offer down. He said, "Foth, you goofed. You should've accepted. I would have given you the details and we'd have split the fee."

Nick Auf der Maur

Where did "Dr. Foth" come from? I did not, as might be imagined, make it up myself.

The nickname came about years back through the inventive mischief of Nick Auf der Maur, the legendary Montreal boulevardier who smoked himself to death, succumbing in early 1998 at the ridiculous age of fifty-five.

Nick qualified for *The Guinness Book of Records*, since he was the only person on earth who was both thrown in jail (and never charged) under Pierre Trudeau's War Measures Act and later ran for mayor of Montreal, an adventure interrupted by being arrested for urinating in an alley behind his favourite pub, which didn't help his campaign.

Through his column in Montreal's *Gazette*, Nick absolutely owned the city. His quixotic role in politics as a meandering figure on the city council further enhanced his eccentric fame. He even ran once as a Conservative candidate for Brian Mulroney, who was a friend, as was Conrad Black. Nick was the first to predict the scandal of the Big Owe, Mayor Jean Drapeau's $1-billion Olympic Stadium folly, where the gravel trucks rolled into the construction site, collected their fees from the tollgate, drove through unloaded, and went around the block to come in again.

In my Ottawa days Nick began to refer to me as "Dr. Foth" in his columns. I never asked him why, but I presumed it was an allusion to Dr. Hunter S. Thompson, the crazed American who invented "gonzo journalism" and once, when the press secretary for presidential candidate Hubert Horatio Humphrey lied to him — as all press secretaries are paid to do — went up to the man's hotel room and set fire to his door.

For years, when I walked Montreal streets, total strangers yelled out, "Hi, Dr. Foth!" — a testimony to the grip and reach Auf der Maur had on that great town that was once the most interesting stop in North America until the insane separatist dreamers ruined its economy, zip, and importance.

The only embarrassing fallout concerning Auf der Maur's nickname for me is that there really is an authentic Dr. Foth — my younger brother, Jack, who worked for fourteen years in the United States through night school and summer school to get his Ph.D. in education. On his trips across the border, Dr. John Fotheringham, now a retired superintendent of schools in Washington, isn't amused by the fake degree conferred on me by the dear, departed Nick.

Cast of Characters

Paul Martin, Jr.

One day in February 1984, just before Pierre Trudeau took his celebrated late-night walk in the snow outside 24 Sussex Drive to decide if he wanted to remain prime minister, I received — as most columnists do from time to time — an anonymous phone call.

The voice — I still don't know whose it was — said, "Watch out, Fotheringham, Paul Martin, Jr., is going for the Liberal leadership." Then the voice hung up.

I'm not sure I even knew at the time that there was someone called Paul Martin, Jr. (having known his daddy well). So I checked him out — Power Corporation, Canada Steamship Lines — and ran a blind item in my column suggesting a Paul Martin, Jr., might be sniffing at the leadership of the Grits.

Weeks later I was striding out of the Ritz-Carlton in Montreal when a couple approached me. "You're Fotheringham?" the male inquired.

I gave him my standard smartass answer: "Depends on whether you're gonna kick me or kiss me."

"Brian Mulroney has warned me about you," the man said. "He says you invent politicians, puff them up, blow them up like a large balloon, and then stick a pin in them."

"Of course," I said, "that's how I make a living."

"Come with me," Paul Martin instructed.

After we drove his wife, Sheila, home, he took me up to his office — this now being midnight — and opened a bottle of Scotch. From that day on Paul and I were friends — as much as the perilous role of journalism can allow a scribbler to become a semi-friend of a politician.

Paul explained that he couldn't make up his mind — having made a fortune, obviously — whether to go into politics or follow a dream to help the African colonies the British Empire had deserted. I thought at the time that a forty-something millionaire who couldn't make up his mind wasn't really an ideal politician.

In my long study of that peculiar animal, the politician, the only thing I know is that Richard Nixon, Joe Clark, and Brian Mulroney all announced to their high school mates at age seventeen that they planned to be president or prime minister, and they all achieved that goal. Someone who was torn between politics and saving the natives in Africa, I didn't quite understand.

I was then living in Ottawa and frequently visited Montreal on weekends, accepting invitations to dinner at Martin's home where he told me again and again how he agonized over African poverty and whether he should be there to help. Paul's indecision way back then showed why he well earned the reputation once in 24 Sussex Drive of being Mr. Dithers.

So I was further amused to see in the *Globe and Mail* some fine digging by two of the paper's Ottawa staff. They revealed how two young Liberal acolytes, Terrie O'Leary and David Herle, on reading my blind column item drove from Ottawa to Montreal to check out this mysterious candidate to make sure he wasn't "a political dud." The two acolytes became the major stickhandlers for the future prime minister. They were also there when Martin ultimately lost to Stephen Harper in the 2006 federal election.

In the 2011 election, as we all know, the Liberal Party was obliterated. Prior to that it was splintered at best between the Martinites and the Chrétienites. The reason J. Chrétien hates P. Martin, beside the fact that the former is the eighteenth of nineteen children born in the Quebec bush, only nine of them surviving infancy, is that he fought his way up through forty years in Parliament, while the Montreal millionaire floated into the Cabinet.

I once asked Martin, in a long interview in his office, how old he was when he became — after spending a university summer as an oil rigger in Alberta and becoming connected with Power Corporation's Maurice Strong — a millionaire. He looked at the ceiling and said, "Oh, I think about thirty."

Another reason Chrétien detests Martin is because he thinks the latter is so indecisive as to be weak, which led to the arcane occasion when Martin, driving back to Ottawa from his Quebec farm, learned on his car radio that he'd been fired as finance minister.

Ever the consummate politician with a perfect memory, Paul Martin knows my son, Brady, was once involved with the Young Liberals in Vancouver. Every time I see Paul, he asks, "How's Brady?"

In 2000, when Martin was finance minister, I was at his table for the Politics and the Pen dinner with his friends and their wives, namely, Robert Brown (head of Bombardier at the time); Ed Lumley, a close friend from childhood days in Windsor; and the new kid on the block, Robert Milton, then head of Air Canada. A good time was had by all that evening.

I was at the *Globe and Mail* at the time, and because of our "friendship," he granted me several long two-page interviews. After he became prime minister, I saw him at a social occasion and asked when we could do the next interview. "Allan," he said, "for you anytime."

Time passed, and at another social occasion at the governor general's residence in Ottawa, I asked the same question and he answered the same thing: "Allan, for you anytime." On the third occasion he shuffled me off to an aide standing behind him with a notebook. Silence remained.

While Martin was prime minister, I never did get an interview.

The best description of Paul Martin comes from Doug Fisher, the elderly sage of the Ottawa Press Gallery. He says: "Do you ever notice that when Paul Martin smiles, his eyes don't?"

P.S. to Paul: Brady has been in Seoul, South Korea, for ten years on a contract teaching English and writing books. Hope he's gonna tell the truth.

Jimmy Pattison

For years Jack Wasserman had the best-read daily column in the *Vancouver Sun* — for an obvious reason. Instead of being tucked away on an inside page, it had an unusual and brilliant placing. It was at the bottom of the front page of the second section. Easy to find, easy to read.

Jack wrote the column in a Hollywood gossip style, with lots of items, all separated by three dots, all the names of his subjects in boldface. One of his favourite subjects was Jimmy Pattison, a Vancouver car dealer and obviously a close friend of his. At that point in time I had never met Pattison.

In 1968, Wasserman suddenly abandoned the most popular position in the paper for the money and fame of a television spot. Later in the year I inherited his storied space and soon received a phone call from Pattison's office, inviting (ordering?) me to his office for lunch. Pattison spent the whole meal questioning me. Married? Children? Education? Ambitions, if any? I told him I would like to go to Spain and write the great Canadian novel. "And what would that cost?" he asked. I threw out the wild and crazy amount of $50,000 but couldn't even think of it with a wife and a young family to raise. I found his questions quite strange and puzzling.

Two weeks later I received in the mail an envelope from Pattison's office. It contained only two things: two cheques, signed by Pattison, each made out for $25,000. One was labelled "Promotion." The other was titled "Public Relations."

I was stunned. I couldn't figure out what this princely sum was for! I put the envelope in a safe place and never gave it a thought again.

In the forty-three years since, I've bumped into Jimmy Pattison untold dozens of times at Vancouver cocktail parties and Toronto business occasions as the car dealer rose to the top of the corporate heap. He has said the small hello and moved swiftly on. He has never once mentioned the envelope.

Among other things, Jimmy owns the world's bestselling copyrighted book, now called *Guinness World Records*, which is sold in more than a hundred countries in thirty-seven languages. In the spring of 2011, *Forbes* magazine listed the annual dollar figures of the globe's billionaires. In Canada, Pattison at eighty-three is one of the richest individuals in the land. The Thomsons are number one, the Westons are number two, and Pattison is tied with the Irvings at number three.

Pattison's total worth is $4 billion. And he still has his $50,000.

Daryl Duke

Daryl Duke was a genius. He was a director and producer from Vancouver but made his mark in Los Angeles with his stunning miniseries *The Thornbirds*. In Vancouver, Daryl owned CKVU-TV. He invented Laurier LaPierre, Pia Southam, and myself as hosts of *The Vancouver Show*, a two-hour magazine program that aired at dinnertime and made us national figures (see photo on page 76).

Duke invited Hunter S. Thompson, the famed gonzo journalist, to come up from Colorado for the show, advertised it, and UBC kids demanded so many tickets that we had to rent bleachers for the studio. Pia and I went to meet Thompson at the airport where Hunter — already blistered on drugs — had been arrested for bringing illegal weapons into Canada, having bought huge knives in the Denver airport.

We got him out of that, me racing to CKVU to warn of trouble ahead, Pia rushing to the Bayshore Inn to get him into his room, push him into the bathroom, and order him to take a shower to sober up. He did, but with only one problem. He forgot to take his suit off.

At the planned hour-long interview Thompson only grunted and didn't answer any questions. The handsome young interviewer, who had fought for the job, was drenched within fifteen minutes in sweat, somewhat resembling the star. It wasn't a great night for live television.

Jack Webster

There are some characters you can't invent. Not the wildest fiction writer could think them up. The Oatmeal Savage was one of them.

Jack Webster absolutely owned the British Columbia airwaves with his CKNW open-mike show. He opened it at 9:00 a.m. *precisely* each morning, by that time having finished his first twenty-cigarette pack of the day.

More than two decades earlier a doctor peered down Jack's throat to his lungs and said it was like gazing into the bottom of a Welsh coal mine. "Go away," he told Webster. "There's nothing I can do for you."

I was once with Jack in a Winnipeg restaurant when he set fire to a waiter. He was flailing his arms during one of his typically outrageous stories and knocked over the flambé cart. "I could have saved him," Webster confessed later, "but I was wearing a new suede jacket."

Just as Walter Cronkite used to be judged in polls as the most trustworthy American figure, the dropout kid from the Glasgow waterfront was for decades the most trusted figure in British California by the Great Unwashed at the other end of the radio dial.

Haggis McBagpipe, as I called him, left school at fourteen for three jobs: delivering milk in the morning and racing between copy boy slots at two newspapers. To qualify for cub reporter status in the National Union of Journalists, he read Charles Dickens and William Shakespeare on the streetcar each day. Right to the end he constantly corrected grammatical mistakes in the conversations of his more educated drinking companions.

Jack had a very good war, ending up a major in Ethiopia. One of his better yarns — once the time frame for the Official Secrets Act had expired — was being seconded for his famed shorthand speed to be the recorder at a court-martial of eighteen British and Australian officers at British Army headquarters in Cairo. The officers had been lonely in the desert and had established romantic, um, relationships with sheep.

Webster was in Ottawa one day and suddenly remembered it was his sixty-fifth birthday. In his usual tumultuous, non-stop rounds, he told every politician and journalist he ran into to come to his hotel room for a celebratory drink. So many eager suppliants showed up that they had to stand on chairs because there was no room left on the floor.

Embarrassed that he couldn't take them all out for dinner, Webster called for room service and ordered up club sandwiches. As the mob grew even thicker, he phoned down and ordered the sandwiches to be cut into smaller portions.

A young blond woman expired on the bed, while a well-known host then on CTV offered a chest massage that was more enthusiastic than required. Fearing scandal, Webster wailed, "Here I am on my sixty-fifth birthday, attempting to get a *woman* out of my bed!" The room service bill came to $887.

Jack was, first on *This Hour Has Seven Days* and later on *Front Page Challenge*, the rare combination of a superb reporter who was also a natural showbiz ham. With those two skills he became the highest-paid working journalist in the country without having to move to dreaded Toronto. He made $300,000 a year in days when that was actually serious money. In doing so he helped the rest of us scribblers. It's called salary creep.

Marjorie Nichols

In the 1970s the three of us ran Vancouver. There was me with my *Vancouver Sun* daily column, Marjorie Nichols with her column in the same paper from the B.C. legislature in Victoria, and barrel-voiced Jack

Webster, who commanded the entire province with his CKNW radio hotline.

We travelled together, ate together, drank together, and caused a sensation when we walked together into any political gathering anywhere. I liked what *Time* said about me: "Canada's most consistently controversial newspaper columnist. A tangier critic of complacency has rarely appeared in a Canadian newspaper." But I liked even better the letter to the editor: "He is the greatest cobweb blower and guff remover in Canadian journalism."

Marj, a product of Red Deer, Alberta, feared neither man nor beast and frightened every politician she ever met. Webster, a refuge from Glasgow, was the loudest voice in any room or bar and never let the lack of a higher education impair his gift of dominating any conversation he had with anyone.

Ms. Nichols, who was a heavy drinker, died in 1991 at the insane age of forty-six, but not before finishing, with the aid of her friend Jane O'Hara, *Mark My Words: The Memoirs of a Very Political Reporter*. And she gave a near heart attack (by not mentioning names) to every powerful male in British Columbia with this passage:

> God, if I were to tell you whom I've slept with, you'd fall off a chair. A lot of them are still in public life. Obviously, there were some people in journalism, but there were a lot of politicians too. I've slept with the husbands of some of my friends. Hell, I've even slept with senators. I never kept count, but I guess I had at least twenty-five such relationships. There's nothing really of interest to tell.
>
> If these had been affairs, or if I had discovered all sorts of state secrets from these public people, that would be one thing. But these were simply animalistic things that took place after long bouts of drinking. It wasn't really fun, though sometimes it seemed like fun. I think sex is highly overrated. A lot of these people were friends, and it didn't change our friendships. But, frequently, after one of these encounters, I'd say, "Why the hell did I do that?"

Boy from Nowhere

I first met Marjorie in the National Press Gallery in Ottawa. She was the second woman to be given membership. Marjorie had gone to the University of Idaho and was a whirlwind on wheels. She was afraid of absolutely no one, and to prove it she outdrank and outsmoked all the boys in the gallery.

She and I became friends, and I introduced her to Jack Webster. The three of us became a rollicking trio, and Doug Fisher, the dean of the Press Gallery, took her aside one day and said, "You've been hanging around Fotheringham and Webster too much. Watch out. One of them is a fake and the other is a phony."

To this day, I don't know which is which. I asked Fisher one day because I was amused by the description and wanted him to tell me which was which. He changed the subject, and I'm still as ignorant today.

Marjorie Nichols giving advice to John Turner while I listen.

Cast of Characters

One day we had a party in Ottawa at the home of Laverne Barnes, and Marjorie left rather pixilated the next morning and forgot her nightie. Laverne, knowing that Marjorie was going to Vancouver the next day, asked a reporter friend who was also going there to drop the nightie at my house, since I would be seeing Marjorie that night. Laverne got my street number slightly wrong, and a stately Vancouver judge who never spoke to me answered the door to the reporter from Ottawa, who said to him, "Here's Marjorie's nightie."

Allan and Sallye Fotheringham and the little Fothlets were sitting around having dinner that night when the doorbell rang. At the door was the distinguished justice from up the street, holding aloft Marjorie's nightie. "Mr. Fotheringham," he said, "I presume this is yours."

In her book Marjorie described what happened when W.A.C. Bennett decided to step down as Social Credit leader and resign his seat in Okanagan South:

> This paved the way for his son to run. So it was with great anticipation that we all flew up to Kelowna for the by-election for Wacky's old seat.
>
> It was going to be an interesting race. Derril Warren, the Conservative leader, was running against Bill Bennett. We sent up a big crew from the *Sun* to cover the event. The *Vancouver Sun* in those days was like the *New York Times*. Boy, when we moved out, money was no object. We hired planes and limousines and you named it. We were all staying at the famous Herb Capozzi–owned Capri, and some legendary parties went on there …
>
> There was a knock on my door. It was Foth. He said, "Hey, Marj-Parge, you got to get me a beer. I've only got another hour to file and I'm all out."
>
> I said: "Where do you expect me to get one of those?"
>
> He said: "Well, you're inventive." And he went back to his room.
>
> I remembered that the night before there had been a big party in the room next to me. I figured out they

probably had left some booze behind. The problem was that I was on the eighth floor of the hotel, and the only way of getting into that room was to swing from my balcony over to the next one.

I thought, oh well, anything for a good cause. So I swung over to this other balcony, clearly risking my life. The balcony door was ajar, and I could see a whole bunch of bottles and empties. I walked right in, gathered up the whole load of them and scooted up to Foth's room.

When I told him what had happened, all he said to me was: "God. How'd you get back over the balcony carrying all those bottles?"

I said: "Surprise, Allan. Doors tend to open from the inside."

Marjorie writes that she missed her flight:

Later, I was in the coffee shop and this old couple came over and said, "Are you Marjorie Nichols?"

I said I was, and they said, "We want to shake your hand."

I said: "Oh, for what?"

They said: "There's a gentleman in the bar telling everybody about the trapeze act you did to get him a beer."

That was Fotheringham, of course. After that he always called me the Bird Woman of Red Deer.

Roy Peterson

Roy Peterson and I were partners on the back page of *Maclean's* for twenty-seven years. No matter what part of the world I was in, Roy and I would have a telephone conversation to discuss the column so he could create the black-and-white drawing that would be in the centre of the column and become a favourite of readers. Many times I just had an idea but hadn't really formulated the column in my head. But, with an idea, Roy would hit the mark dead on every time.

On the tenth anniversary of the back page, Roy called me up and suggested a reunion in Chicago … just we two. I agreed. Off I went to the Tremont Hotel, which Roy had arranged. We had a great weekend together — just the two of us, or so I thought. I later found out he had brought his wife, Margaret. But she was doing her own thing in the background. I never saw her once. When I checked out of the hotel, I was told that my bill had already been taken care of.

On the twentieth anniversary of the back page, I received another call from Roy. How about this time we take our wives with us and go to Las Vegas? Roy would arrange everything. Off Anne and I went to the opulent Bellagio Hotel in Vegas. When we arrived, there was a basket in our room put together by Roy and Margaret with gifts, a booklet outlining our itinerary, and a bottle of champagne. Shows, fine dining, a helicopter ride over Las Vegas, even gold earrings for our wives followed. Once again, when I checked out of the hotel, the bill had been taken care of by Roy.

Roy Peterson always knows how to draw me.

Boy from Nowhere

In a video put together when I was given the Bruce Hutchinson Lifetime Achievement Award at the Jack Webster Awards dinner in Vancouver, Roy stated that I was a true gentleman. Wrong. Roy was the true gentleman.

He couldn't be touched by any other cartoonist in Canada, winning seven National Newspaper Awards for his work in the *Vancouver Sun*. Roy has the distinguished feature of having in his career only one cartoon "killed" by a squeamish editor — the one picturing the famously fearless Pierre Trudeau cowering in a corner.

As Roy used to boast, he carried me on his back for twenty-seven years in *Maclean's*. He has a point.

28
Life Is a Series of Memories

Life is a collection of memories. They pile up, connect together, disconnect, and make in a scrambly way what life is all about.

1. Having a double bubble in the bathtub at Adare Manor, a castle that is now rated the top hotel and golf resort in Ireland but was also the ancestral home of my wife's ancestors. Double bubble, of course, being a bubble bath while drinking champagne.

2. Going to the Turks and Caicos Club Med and becoming the oldest guest at Club Med to swing on the flying trapeze. I was seventy-one at the time.

As of 2004, I am the oldest person to fly on the trapeze at Club Med. Shortly after, I left for Doug Creighton's funeral.

3. Going to my neighbour Ian Graham's home for a charades party with my tennis buddies from the Toronto Lawn Tennis Club. I pulled out from the hat "The Joy of Sex." How does one do charades for "The Joy of Sex"? They didn't get it, but I had fun trying.

4. Throwing a birthday party for Beth Currie, who requested karaoke for the entertainment. To get things going, my wife, Anne, sang and danced to "New York, New York" while in top hat, fish-net stockings, and tails. It brought the house down.

5. Seeing my son, Brady, on a poster for Epilepsy Toronto. It showed him on his mountain bike while taking the Silk Road. I was at the St. Lawrence Market in Toronto when I unexpectedly came upon it. I was so proud.

6. Visiting Lana Underhill's home in Languedoc, France. While Lana and Anne were out to the market, I put on a fire. Upon their return, the whole house was covered in ash and smoke. I'm a sensitive poet. What do I know about building a fire?

7. Sitting with the lieutenant governor of Saskatchewan, Linda Haverstock, during the convocation ceremonies after getting my honorary degree from the University of Saskatchewan. We sat there and counted the number of graduates who had on jeans and sandals under their graduation gowns.

8. Dancing during one of Allan Slaight and Emmanuelle Gattuso's fabulous Christmas parties to the tune of "Mr. Cellophane" from the musical *Chicago*. I received a standing ovation.

9. Visiting John and Sandra Ferguson in Chantilly, France, where they were living while John was working for the Aga Khan. Upon arrival we had a bottle of champagne, a French tradition I quite like and could get used to.

10. Riding a donkey on the beach at Acapulco, and after getting off, the donkey giving me a kick. How ungrateful. I had given his minder a healthy tip.

11. Being invited to Klosters in Switzerland by Norman Jewison and his future wife, Lynne St. David. I took the lift to the first hill and proceeded down to wrap myself around the larger-than-life inflated snowman balloon. Time for the chalet.

12. Skiing out at Whistler and falling head first into a snowbank. Anne thought I had broken my neck. She started digging and yelling, "Are you okay? Say something!"

    I replied, "Leave me alone. I'm searching for avalanche victims!"

13. Being introduced to Ajijic, Mexico, by Herb and Ildiko Marshall, only to find friends from Ottawa days, Rob Parker and his lovely wife, Terry Keleher, who are permanent residents of Ajijic. Rob is referred to as "The Mayor."

14. Being part of the winning team in 2009 at the annual Bowen Island Tennis Classic. I have the winning cup to prove it.

15. Speaking at a seminar in Jamaica as the Canadian representative to the Georgetown University Leadership Group out of Washington, D.C.

16. Richard Addis and I in Memphis, Tennessee, at the Lennox Lewis–Mike Tyson fight. Crowds jammed the streets, so Richard and I got into a horse-drawn carriage and asked the driver to get through the mob to our hotel. A wheel of the carriage caught the door of the limo filled with Tyson's bodyguards and tore it off. Mayhem. Our lady driver whipped the horse, yelled "Yeehaw!" and galloped through the horde, leaving the limo in the dust. The editor and the number one columnist of the *Globe and Mail* were saved again.

17. Kip and Jennifer announcing at the end of Anne's and my West Coast wedding celebration that they were expecting our first grandchild.

18. Holding our first grandchild.

19. Holding every one of our grandchildren.

20. Locking myself out of Keith Spicer's fancy flat in Paris while chasing Mendès, his cat. I threw Mendès in and pulled the door shut before realizing what I had done. What was a man to do while waiting for Anne or Spicer to return? Head to the nearby café and sip champagne.

21. Going with my son, Kip, to a Notre Dame University game in South Bend, Indiana, courtesy of Mike and Bernie Wadsworth (Mike having been the director of athletics for Notre Dame). At the end of the weekend Kip announced that Notre Dame was where his children were going to go to university. Impressed?

22. Going to the colourful and theatrical funeral of one of the kings of Bali. We sat with the dignitaries and watched the cremation while wearing saris.

23. Having my hat catch fire while dancing with Anne and performing the Saskatchewan Dip at the Regent Hotel in Hong Kong during the 1997 Hong Kong handover.

24. Going to Cinquante Cinq, the famous French restaurant on the beach just outside St. Tropez for the first time. Not the last.

25. Staying at Roy and Rae Heenan's home in Gassin in the south of France. What a treasure. And seeing in the guest books the famous people who have had the pleasure of staying there, as well — everyone from TV news anchor Knowlton Nash to Pierre Elliott Trudeau and his sons. May we go back, Roy?

26. Winning the consolation prize at the first annual Kelowna Celebrity Tennis Classic organized by Wally Lightbody. That was before I got my new knee.

27. Kip running to La Croix Valmer and back, two and a half miles from Gassin, to get his old man an English newspaper.

28. Picnicking on American Island in Georgian Bay with Jim and Brenda McCutcheon, along with Anna and Julian Porter, the day before Catherine Porter and Graeme Burt's wedding ceremony at Camp Hurontario.

29. Singing "Royal Britannia" while having Pimm's with all of the drunken Brits after leaving the Royal Enclosure at Ascot and seeing the queen off.

In my top hat and morning suit in the Royal Enclosure at Ascot. Anne loved the ladies' hats.

30. Prince Philip roaring with laughter over my column he had read that morning in the newspaper before meeting me on the royal yacht *Britannia*.

31. Heli-skiing above Whistler Mountain, making it down one slope, and spending the rest of the day in the helicopter while Anne skied. Later that evening when I received a certificate stating I'd heli-skied, I asked, "Do I get frequent-flyer points?"

32. Having my face put on a WANTED poster on Bowen Island when the locals didn't like one of my columns.

WANTED

Known as "Dr. Foth" *aka* Dr. Froth. *aka*   Allan Fotheringham

Character: very shallow Toronto type

Occupation: chitchat columnist & obituary writer for the *Grope & Rail*

Crimes: Hangs out at Hood Point with other Hoodlums during summer months and throws annual birthday party that he shamelessly brags about to all and sundry. Carries sharp pencils but misses the point. Publishes annual nasty article about his pathetic little summer vacation on Bowen Island. We, the good citizens of Bowen Island say he should get a life and get lost. We never want Fotheringham to belittle or besmirch Bowen Island again, so please report any sightings of this conceited scoundrel to the local constabulary.

He will be transported to the Continent immediately.

33. Going to Senator Pat Carney and Paul White's wedding on Saturna Island. When the speeches were given, every time Paul White's name was uttered, the crowd yelled, "Never heard of him!"

34. Sitting on Ernest Hemingway's bar stool in a Havana bar and ordering a mojito.

35. Taking Anne to two inaugurations — Clinton's and Dubya's. Hillary and Laura were thrilled to see us on both occasions.

36. Going to the Fantastic Palm Springs Follies and the MC, who was Canadian, yelling from the stage, "The famous writer Allan Fotheringham is with us this evening. Allan, aren't you dead yet?"

37. Going to the funeral of John Phillips (of the 1960s The Mamas & the Papas) in Palm Springs to get material for a column. Judy Kerr heard we were going to a funeral and said, "They haven't been in Palm Springs long enough to know anyone who's died and go to their funeral."

38. Sitting in the back of a truck heading to the horse stables at the Kentucky Downs with Kathleen Tynan, the wife of British critic Kenneth Tynan. I thought I'd died and gone to heaven.

39. When Tom Axworthy called Paul Manning to tell him that Pierre Trudeau had taken a walk in the snow and was going to resign, Manning was sworn to secrecy. He immediately called and told me the news. I was the first to know.

40. Jack Webster meeting Paul Manning for the first time.

    Webster to Manning: "Married?"

    The reply: "No."

    Webster: "Queer?"

41. Receiving my honorary degree at the University of New Brunswick, and Kip along with his eight-month pregnant wife, Jennifer, coming to New Brunswick to be there.

42. Having dinner with my aged mother and journalist Craig Oliver. Craig explained to my mother that his mother gave him the best advice to get a girl: make the girls laugh. My mother asked who he decided on in the end. "Why the one who gave the best blow job." My mother looked down at her soup. To her dying day she always asked me how my friend Craig was.

43. Visiting Paul Manning and his wife in Carlsbad, New Mexico, and when leaving, Manning hanging on to my car, Big Blue. He kept on talking, his wife hanging on to him, and was still talking as I put the car into third gear. I think he might have wanted to come with us.

44. In 1983 I was unprepared to give a speech in Calgary at the Canadian Bar Association, Saskatchewan Branch. My fellow speaker, prominent lawyer Maurice Schumiacher, asked if I wanted to see his speech. I did and then asked if he minded if I went first. No problem. I proceeded to give his speech only in the reverse of what he was going to say. Needless to say, he was more than angry. And to think I got paid for that speech.

45. Watching my grandsons, Hunter and Angus, playing hockey. It reminded me of watching my own sons play hockey when they were young.

46. Seeing my grandson, Lachlan, dazzle the girls in his kindergarten class. Chip off the old block? Chip off the older block?

47. Being taken out of the hospital to go to my seventy-fifth birthday party at Charles Pachter's art studio. I don't remember a thing about that party.

48. Throwing out the first pitch at Nat Bailey Stadium in Vancouver when the Vancouver Canadians played against the Spokane Indians.

49. The look on my grandson Lachlan's face when I gave him the baseball I used for that first pitch.

50. The joy of my grandchildren closing around me to blow out the birthday candles on my birthday cake while I cried.

51. Sitting in the rooftop bar of the Caravelle Hotel (nicknamed the Hanoi Hilton) in Saigon, having a drink with journalists David Halberstam of the *New York Times*, Malcolm Browne of United Press

I threw the first pitch at Nat Bailey Stadium in 2009 when the Vancouver Canadians (owned by buddy Jake Kerr) played the Spokane Indians.

International, and Bob Woodward of the *Washington Post*, and telling war stories during the Vietnam War. All (except me) won Pulitzer Prizes later.

52. Jim Coutts buying a piano and nicknaming it "Dr. Foth" so his friends could come over and "have a tinkle on Foth."

53. Entering the Canadian embassy in Rome for the first time to find a magnificent building overlooking the hills of Rome accompanied by a swimming pool and tennis courts among gorgeous gardens. And to think I turned down the possibility of being the ambassador, as suggested by Brian Mulroney. So much for journalistic integrity.

54. Seeing Secretariat run his last race at Woodbine Racetrack on October 23, 1973.

55. (Now Senator) Pamela Wallin presenting a speech at my sixty-fifth birthday party at Biagio Ristorante and stating that I was "a pitiful lay." How does *she* know?

56. Anne and I meeting Ontario Premier Dalton McGuinty for the first time. When I introduced her as my wife, he shook her hand and said, "You have my sympathy."

57. Introducing Anne to Brian Mulroney at a luncheon at the Sheraton Centre in Toronto. His response: "What are you doing with this jerk?"

58. Introducing Anne to Jean Chrétien at the York Club and having him comment: "You have my condolences."

59. Walking my daughter down the aisle. I was so proud.

60. Discussing soccer scores at lunch with Phillip Crawley, the British publisher of the *Globe and Mail*.

61. Seeing the poker club playing cards in the chapel on the ship to Antarctica because there was nowhere else for them to play.

62. The story of the Arab sheik who donated a $1,000,000 stallion to the stables for stud in Port Stanley in the Falkland Islands. He was appalled at the quality of the horses racing, which only occurred two days in a year: Boxing Day and the day after Boxing Day.

63. Marilyn Freer telling a group of people at a cocktail party while in Budapest, "Foth's idea of foreplay is walking into a room."

64. At the *Vancouver Sun* when I was new and Simma Holt, a fellow reporter, bringing up in the freight elevator and into the newsroom a baby elephant from a visiting circus. It went crazy and destroyed typewriters along with everything else in its way.

65. Charles Taylor, then editor of the McGill University newspaper, and I, then editor of the University of British Columbia newspaper, while

at a Canadian University Press conference for campus papers in Toronto, dropping beer cases full of water out the window of the Royal York Hotel to see if we could hit the streetcars. The police knocked at the door. End of party.

66. Sondra Gotlieb refusing to seat me beside Kathleen Tynan at a Canadian embassy dinner in Washington because she knew I found Kathleen interesting.

67. John Ralston Saul arriving off a plane to a party in Ottawa and looking somewhat dishevelled. Val Sears, the Ottawa bureau chief for the *Toronto Star* and host of the evening, yelled, "John, why didn't you get a freshly ironed shirt? Adrienne's family has been in the business for years!"

68. Dalton Camp taking credit on page 22 of his book *Points of Departure* for the statement that is now part of the Canadian psyche due to my column on the back page of *Maclean's*: "Subscribers now read their national magazine from back to front."

69. Meeting at a party in Little Rock, Arkansas, the head fundraiser for Bill Clinton's presidential campaign. When asked his opinion of the campaign, which was at the halfway point then, he replied: "That's easy. Dole is dead and Clinton is in heat again!"

70. My brother, Jack, and I being thrown off the school bus and continuing our wrestling in a ditch while the bus drove on. Our ongoing upmanship continues to this day, only it is now verbal wrestling.

71. Watching *Singin' in the Rain* and thinking when I come back in another life I want to be either an architect or Gene Kelly. Boy, do I love to dance.

72. Being at Minette Ross's for dinner and doing the Saskatchewan Dip with her. I accidently dropped her on the floor with me on top of her. Anne turned to Gerry Charney, another guest, and calmly said, "Time to take him home."

73. On Lamu Island, Kenya, sitting on a sandspit the whole day with my son, Kip, and reading and passing articles back and forth in the sun. Kip later told me that was the day he realized he was his father's son.

74. Driving my car Old Blue across the continent from Vancouver to Washington, D.C., with my buddy Marsha Erb. We stopped at Mom's Restaurant in Denver and struck up a conversation with Les, a local. Les had a number of rifles. I asked if he had a handgun. Les replied, "No, but I aims to get me one."

75. After my serious and near-fatal illness, I wrote a letter to my sister, Irene. In my recognizable scrawl on a single sheet of paper, it read: "I'm back!"

What life is all about is a collection of memories.

29
Fothisms

Regressive Conservatives
Pierre Easily Trendeau
Pierre Elliott Reincarnation
Ottawa, Sparta of the Tundra
    Ennui on the Rideau
    The Town That Fun Forgot
    Yesterday's City, Tomorrow
British California
    Bennett Columbia, Lotusland, Wacky Bennett, Mini Wac, Wonky A.
    Bombast
Phyling Phil Gaglardi
Valium West
Snafouver
Hongcouver
Vancouver Land of the Hot Tub
John Chancellor — G8 Trudeau
Myron Baloney
Wimsy
Da Preem
The Jaw That Walked Like a Man
Canadian Broadcorping Castration
Toronto — The Big Pickle
Haggis McBagpipe, the Oatmeal Savage
The Excited States of America
City Dedicated to Mammon
Air Arrogance the Liberal Campaign Jet
Somewhere over Moose Jaw
The Granite Curtain (Rockies)
The Tweed Curtain (Oak Bay, British Columbia)

Boy from Nowhere

The Brogue That Walks and Talks Like a Man (Jack Webster)
The Natural Governing Party (Liberals)
The Holy Mother Corp (CBC)
Jurassic Clark (Joe Clark)
Joe Clark from Bravado
Joe Clark from Cautious
Joe If

30
The First Page Last

I have just received a call from Doug. He tells me the lads — Ted, Tom K., Tom S., Chris, George, Ken, John C., and John D. — want to know if the book is finished as they want me to play in the geezer tennis round robin. A memoir of one's life is never finished. There is always more that could be written. As one says in the industry, it's not what you put in, it's what you leave out.

On top of that, I don't have time to play in the round robin this week. I'm chasing a story, and as stated to Bob Lewis those many years ago, I have to stick with the story. However, so you don't feel at loose ends, I thought I'd pull out my first column on the back page of *Maclean's*, dated October 6, 1975. I hope you enjoy it. I'm off to catch a plane!

That Trudeau's Such a Lovely Guy, So Loyal to Those Who Work for Him
Column by Allan Fotheringham

The British have a love word called *nouse*. Nouse means intelligence combined with common sense. Horse sense. It is useless having a burnished intellect that sends out its own pure beam of light if there is no sense attached to it at the lower end. The lack of nouse is the outstanding feature of the Trudeau government.

People with nouse do not grant themselves 33½ percent pay increases while attempting to exhort the grubby unwashed to a policy of restraint. People with nouse do not slip back into arrogance, with the ease of pulling on fireplace slippers, as soon as they achieve majority government once again. People with nouse do not insult the public with the cynical payoff to a prime minister's principal secretary, rewarding forty-three-year-old Jack Austin's fifteen months of service by giving him a lifetime guaranteed income in the Senate — thirty-two future years at $29,300 per for a total of $937,600.

Boy from Nowhere

The nouse-less Trudeaucrats. It is their shining characteristics, their neon-lit trademark. Run your eye down the list of Trudeau ministers and it is the consistent quality that pops up in this uniform cast of technocrats.

The image of automotive technicians who run Ottawa has disguised a remarkable facet of Pierre Trudeau: he lacks the ability to be — in another British political phrase — "a good butcher." He cannot bring himself to prune and hack the congenital stumblers and faint-hearted clots who clutter up his ministry.

It is generally unrecognized that Trudeau (mainly because of the artful change of life he goes through every few years: i.e., the recycled swinger, the reincarnation of Laurier, the homebody and suburbanite daddy) has passed both John Diefenbaker and Lester Pearson in length of service. By the time his current term is up, he will have passed Louis St. Laurent and will be well into the full gallop in pursuit of Mackenzie King (John Turner knows how to count, too). This longevity through three elections (and four mental costume changes) has been established with a cast of characters that drifts on untouched by the supposedly tough hand of Himself. The intellectually rigorous product of Jesuit mental discipline finds himself unable to wield the axe even in the face of proven incompetence, even in the face of his proud boast, when he formed his first ministry, that his ministers would have to "produce or else."

We all believed it at the time. "Nothing is permanent," the new prime minister warned ominously in 1968 when he picked the largest Cabinet in Canadian history, a collection of twenty-nine supposedly nervous souls. Instead, we waited two years for his first Cabinet "shuffle." Where was the chop, the famed Trudeau uncompromising lust for excellence? It produced not a single new face in the Cabinet, with two of the ministers going back to the jobs they held under Pearson.

Ah, the Pearson years. Soft, nice-guy Mike Pearson, who was too kindly and old-shoe to jettison familiar friends. Do you know that Pierre Elliott Idealist has existed for more than seven years with the core of his Cabinet picked by Pearson? He has yet, despite the readjustment forced on him by John Turner's farewell, to put his own stamp on the Cabinet.

After the coitus interruptus in the long-awaited 1970 shuffle, we had to wait four more years before there was a bloodletting. The ruthless one was six years in power in 1974 before sacking *anyone*. At that the only two

228

of any note were the feckless Herb Gray, who has since discovered more bravery outside the Cabinet than he ever did in it, and the handsome Bob Stanbury, terror of the Ottawa stenographic pool.

So what are we left with in 1975? Men who have long since proven their inability to shoulder the burdens thrown them, men who have bent and stretched the Peter Principle to unreasonable limits, men who — even taking into consideration the demands of regional, racial, and religious demands of regional, racial, and religious quotas — have no business surviving in this government.

James Richardson, the poor little rich boy who will live forever in political folklore for Marci McDonald's description of him falling out of his bunk all night on one of his defence ministry ships, because his naval officers "neglected" to tell him to strap himself in.

Judd Buchan, the insensitive prize-winning insurance salesman, unleashed upon the Native people of the land as Minister of Indian Affairs, regarded in the North as a beardless boy attempting to learn as quickly as possible the time-tested Liberal gifts of waffle, shuffle, and mumble.

Can anyone take seriously a government that maintained for seven years dear old Mitchell Sharp, foot-in-mouth Mitchell Sharp, author of the famous reply when asked about the 1968 Russian invasion of Czechoslovakia: "Disappointing."

There are so many: Hugh Faulkner, who always appears as if he would be more comfortable in an Oscar Wilde play. Alastair Gillespie, that interchangeable face, the silver-haired executive from Central Casting who so pleases those interested in industry, trade, and commerce. Robert Andras, the very image of a Northern Ontario service club recording secretary masquerading as a manager of a very important Canadian ministry.

Even the heavies in the Trudeau cabinet have that bloodless, technocrat cast that forces one to look back with fond vigour on such as Judy LaMarsh. There is Marc Lalonde, an honest man who still can't understand what was wrong with Air Seagram, the only man in Ottawa, in the words of the Press Gallery's Marjorie Nichols, "with an IQ of two hundred and the political judgment of Justin." There is Otto Lang, who can never concede he is wrong (as he was on Morgentaler) and who manages the formidable feat of appearing to be to the right even though he is surprisingly progressive.

Can anyone recall a single memorable phrase that will live beyond any of these ministers? Is "eat shit" to survive as the only quotable epitaph of this government? Those who leave, a Hellyer, a Kierans, a Turner, are allowed to sidle away. The strong resign. The weak are never sacked.

It is ironic that Pierre Elliott Trudeau, who came into politics and shook our minds as the greatest individualist within memory, ended up swallowed by the system, whittled down by the machinery, diminished, just another cog unable to move the bureaucratic wheel of party politics. In the art of jaded politics, he is a prime exhibit. He is demeaned. The system of Cabinet tenure, squatters' rights, has not changed. He has changed.

31
Left on the Copy Room Floor

There are a few buttons that get pushed in error other than the "medical button" I previously mentioned. One is the computer button that allows copy to disappear without your knowledge. Hence, some copy doesn't make the book.

But I think you will enjoy these tidbits.

Another Character from the Cast: Bill Clinton

I met President Bill Clinton when he was in Vancouver for the 1997 Asia-Pacific Economic Cooperation (APEC) conference. My friend, Senator Pat Carney, asked if I would escort her to the private cocktail reception before the conference began.

I was going through the receiving line, and there was President Clinton being introduced to the guests by David Anderson, a prominent Liberal in British Columbia. Anderson never liked me, but when he introduced me to the president, he said, "President Clinton, this is Allan Fotheringham, the best-known journalist in the nation."

I then said to Clinton, "Yes, Mr. President, and I'm going to run for prime minister in the next election."

Without missing a beat, Clinton replied, "Good for you, young man!"

Charm drips off his elbow. He can make an audience melt.

Years later I had the opportunity to go through the White House late in the evening accompanied by Jean Sonmor, who was with the *Toronto Sun* at the time. I was amazed at how compact it is and how parts of it are like a rabbit warren. The Oval Office is very small. In fact, I was astonished at how close President Clinton's secretary's desk was to the area where he and Monica Lewinsky carried on with the cigar. Quite "the man."

Boy from Nowhere

From the *Toronto Sun* to Antarctica

One of the rules of the *Toronto Sun* was that after ten years of service everyone got a paid ten-week sabbatical. When my turn came up, one of Doug Creighton's assistants, Lynn Carpenter, called me and said I should take the sabbatical unlike some who ignored it. Coincidentally, at the same time, Sam Blythe of Blythe and Company (a travel business) asked me if I would like to go onto one of his ships to give speeches. This was at the millennium, and the ship was going on a four-month trip around the world. Sam said I was welcome to do the full four months.

I was still writing for *Maclean's* then and felt that four months away from the political scene might be a wee bit much. So I decided that Anne and I would pick up the ship at Rio de Janeiro and take it from there to Buenos Aires, the Falkland Islands, Ushuaia, Argentina, Antarctica, back to Ushuaia, leave the ship and go to Santiago, Chile, Lima, Peru, Machu Picchu, and then finally to the Amazon. The whole trip would take five weeks, and I would write for *Maclean's* along the way.

It was Anne's first cruise, she being prone to motion sickness. It was my second, the first one being, oh, so long ago when I first travelled to Europe as a young man. But the two trips were like night and day.

When we arrived at the ship, Anne noticed carpeting being hoisted onto the vessel and thought this strange, since the ship was supposed to have been completely refitted for its inaugural voyage. After we found our contact, Stephen Richer, he told us that when the passengers arrived in Athens to start their dream millennium cruise the ship hadn't been ready. They were now renovating it in every port. This didn't help the morale of the passengers. My speeches were to do the trick.

I thought up a series entitled "What's Wrong …?" With the United States. With Canada. With England. With the world. And so on. The first lecture was about what was wrong with the United States. I finished my speech by saying: "America ruled the world the last century and the next century will belong to China." Perceptive.

A woman sitting beside Anne in the front row turned to her at the end of the speech and said, "You Canadians don't know anything about Americans. Fuck off!" When we returned to our room, hate mail was shoved under the door. The next morning in the dining room someone posted a notice: BOYCOTT FOTHERINGHAM'S LECTURES. HE HATES AMERICA.

That night, when I concluded the lecture, I said, "My wife doesn't tell me what to think, my wife doesn't write my speeches, as a matter of fact, we don't even vote the same way. Last night, after my speech, a woman seated beside her said something so foul that it cannot be repeated in front of horses or small children. There's just one thing I cannot understand. It's the anger. Thank you."

It turned out that 80 percent of the passengers were Americans. For the next two weeks, every single day, Anne was approached by complete strangers, all Americans, who apologized for the woman's behaviour. The woman didn't come out of her cabin for the rest of the trip. And the next notice that went up on the board stated: I LIKE FOTHERINGHAM'S LECTURES. I THINK IT IS CALLED FREEDOM OF SPEECH. By the next morning, the notice was torn down.

On another evening, while giving my speech, I spotted young children running around the banquettes at the back of the room. Then I noticed they had grouped together and were whispering. The next day the ship coordinator told me there had been complaints from the parents. Apparently, a couple of passengers were at the back, as well, listening to the speech. But that wasn't all they were doing. The woman was "servicing" the man while I was speaking. The children, confused, asked their parents what they were doing. As I said to the coordinator, "I have on occasion had people go to sleep during my speeches, but never have I had anyone listening to me reach sexual ecstasy." So much for improving the morale.

There is more, but I have to stop somewhere. Dr. Foth signing off.

OF RELATED INTEREST

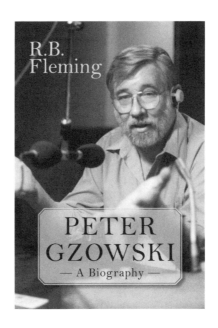

Peter Gzowski
A Biography
by R.B. Fleming
978-1554887200
$40.00

This first definitive biography of Peter Gzowski probes his childhood and follows him through his career, beginning with his days at the University of Toronto's *The Varsity* in the mid-1950s through to his tremendous success on CBC Radio's *Morningside* and his time at the *Globe and Mail*. Featuring a diverse range of black-and-white photographs from Gzowski's past, this book reveals the personal story of one of Canada's most prolific, passionate, and truly patriotic Canadian media personalities.

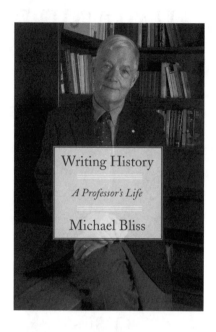

Writing History
A Professor's Life
by Michael Bliss
978-1554889532 | $40.00

One of Canada's best-known and most-honoured historians turns to the raw material of his own life. A university professor, prolific scholar, public intellectual, and frank critic of the world, Michael Bliss describes a life that has taken him from small-town Ontario to international recognition for his books about Canadian and medical history. In this erudite and measured memoir, Bliss reveals his views on personal, public and political history with clarity and grace.

Victor Feldbrill
Canadian Conductor Extraordinaire
by Walter Pitman
978-1554887682 | $40.00

Author Walter Pitman delves into the life and cultural contribution of one of Canada's most talented conductors. Victor Feldbrill was known for his limitless enthusiasm and support of Canadian music and young musicians, as well as for his insistence on playing music by Canadian composers. Starting his career in the Toronto Symphony Orchestra at just eighteen years old, Feldbrill saw his influence and inspiration span from coast to coast, setting the stage for many young Canadian musical talents to come.

Available at your favourite bookseller.
What did you think of this book?
Visit *www.dundurn.com* for reviews, videos, updates, and more!